CLASSIC *f*M

The *Friendly* Guide to

Music

Darren Henley

HODDER
EDUCATION
PART OF HACHETTE UK

The publisher has used its best endeavours to ensure that the URLs for external websites referred to in this book are correct and active at the time of going to press. However, the publisher has no responsibility for the websites and can give no guarantee that a site will remain live or that the content is or will remain appropriate.

For UK order enquiries: please contact Bookpoint Ltd, 130 Milton Park, Abingdon, Oxon OX14 4SB. Telephone: +44(0) 1235 827720. Fax: +44(0) 1235 400454. Lines are open 09.00–17.00, Monday to Saturday, with a 24-hour message answering service. You can also order through our website www.hoddereducation.com

British Library Cataloguing in Publication Data: a catalogue record for this title is available from the British Library.

First published in UK 2006, by Hodder Education, 338 Euston Road, London NW1 3BH.

Typeset by Servis Filmsetting Ltd, Stockport, Cheshire
Printed in Great Britain for Hodder Education, part of Hachette UK, 338 Euston Road, London NW1 3BH, by CPI Cox & Wyman, Reading, Berkshire RG1 8EX.

Hachette UK's policy is to use papers that are natural, renewable and recyclable products and made from wood grown in sustainable forests. The logging and manufacturing processes are expected to conform to the environmental regulations of the country of origin.

Impression number   10 9 8

Year   2010 2009 2008

To Izzy, with the hope that as she grows, her night-time music becomes her day-time music too.

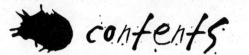 contents

Foreword

I've never been one for treating music as hallowed or sacred. When the brainy kid at school first played me the opening bars of Beethoven's Fifth on a scratchy 78, I didn't drop to my knees in awe. To be frank, it didn't occur to me that it was a particularly different sort of thing from Duke Ellington or John Coltrane or Buddy Holly or any of the other good music I was listening to at that time. I just whooped and shouted, "Isn't that great!" And I feel exactly the same today – Rhapsody in Blue, Ol' Blue Eyes, even Elton John and Blue are all logged in the same big file in my head marked "Great Music *that Everyone Should Hear*." So, when Classic FM approached me to present **The Friendly Guide to Music** – with "no tosh, no twaddle, and

vii

definitely no snobby bits" – I thought – "You bet. This is a job that was made for me!"

The book which accompanies the series aims to tell you enough, but not too much, about lots of different areas of classical music: from what Hildegard wrote when Barbarossa was crowned, to what Hans Zimmer wrote when Nelson Mandela was released. It's not meant to be a learned treatise, but if it makes you curious to read and hear more, then I say, "Isn't that great?"

Tony Robinson

The radio programme based upon this book, also called *The Classic FM Friendly Guide to Music* and presented by Tony Robinson, was the winner of the Gold Medal in the Best Music Programme category of the New York International Radio Broadcasting Awards 2007.

A Friendly Word Before We Get Started

If you are standing in a bookshop reading this, wondering whether to buy a copy of *The Classic FM Friendly Guide to Music*, then please allow us to help you to decide.

If you flick through the next 200 or so pages, you will quickly discover that there are a lot of things that this book is not. It is not the most detailed and learned book about classical music that you will be able to lay your hands on in any high street bookshop. It is not packed full of impenetrable

musicological arguments about contrapuntal syncopation, or microscopic analysis of a long-forgotten composer's unpublished work. In short, it is not going to be much help to you if you are already an expert in the subject, busily researching your PhD thesis.

Instead, this is the book about classical music for everyone else – and especially for people who wouldn't normally consider buying a book on the subject, but who are, nonetheless, interested in developing a greater understanding of classical music.

If that sounds like you, then you will be pleased to hear that, just like Classic FM itself, this book is mercifully free of the jargon that is sometimes associated with the classical music world.

The advent of pop music meant that, for a significant part of the 20th century, classical music came to be regarded as the preserve of a cultural elite. Those people on the inside of the classical club didn't seem to want to share the musical delights that they had discovered with those people who were outside the elite. For people looking in, classical music seemed to be surrounded by an impenetrable ring of steel.

The Three Tenors' concert in Rome during the World Cup finals of 1990 marked a resurgence in

x

popular interest in classical music. The belief that classical music can be enjoyed by everybody, no matter what their age, class or geographical location, is one of the cornerstones upon which Classic FM was founded in 1992. It is an ideal to which we have remained true ever since.

It is worth remembering that classical music was in fact the popular music of its day. In the days before radio, television, the internet and any recordings, what we now consider to be classical music was played live in churches, palaces, coffee houses, concert halls and ordinary homes across Europe. The composers who created it were writing music that would be performed at specific occasions and enjoyed by audiences or congregations far and wide. Music and the arts were regarded as having a civilizing effect on society, whether the particular works were religious or secular in their nature.

So what exactly is classical music?

This is one of the questions that is most often asked of us at Classic FM. The strictest definition of classical music is everything that was written in the Classical period (between 1750 and 1830), but today we understand classical music to be much more than just music written in those 80 years.

Calling a piece of music "classical" is sometimes done as a means of generically distinguishing it from "popular music". One of the major tests of whether a tune is or isn't classical music has traditionally been whether it has a sense of "permanence" about it, in that it was still being performed many years after its composition. This argument begins to fall down as the heritage of pop music becomes ever longer, with hits from the 1950s still being played on the radio today, well over half a century after their original release. It is also hard for us to tell whether a newly written piece of classical music will indeed attain that level of "permanence" in the future.

The *Concise Oxford Dictionary of Music* offers the following as one of its definitions of classical music:

Music of an orderly nature, with qualities of clarity and balance, and emphasising formal beauty rather than emotional expression (which is not to say that emotion is lacking).

It is true to say that much of classical music follows specific rules of style and form, which we will discuss further in Chapters 2–7 of our *Friendly Guide*. However, this definition is still not quite a catch-all.

One of the most striking differences between classical and pop music is the different way the two genres place their emphasis on the relative importance of the composer and the performer. In pop music the performer is all, but in classical music the composer is the star of the show. It is his name that tends to come first in the credits and it is he who is remembered by history. Take Mozart's *Clarinet Concerto in A* as an example. Not many people remember Anton Stadler, the clarinettist for whom it was written, but everyone knows Mozart's name. Conversely, if you ask most music fans whom they would most associate with that hardy perennial *White Christmas*, they would reply "Bing Crosby", rather than the song's composer, Irving Berlin.

Some of those self-appointed members of classical music's ruling elite like to claim that film scores sit outside the world of classical music. Yet, the first dedicated soundtrack was composed by Camille Saint-Saëns for the 1908 film *L'Assassinat du Duc de Guise*. Since then, Copland, Vaughan Williams, Walton, Prokofiev and Shostakovich have all written music for the cinema. If we go back to the time of Beethoven, we find him composing incidental music for the theatre of the day. Had cinema been invented in his life, he would undoubtedly have written this genre of music too. Throughout classical music's history, composers have always written music for those who pay, whether their patrons be rich noblemen or rich film studios.

Today, film soundtracks are among the most popular symphonic works being composed, with pieces by the likes of John Williams, John Barry,

Hans Zimmer, Howard Shore and James Horner providing an excellent gateway into wider listening to classical music.

Whatever the definition of classical music to which you personally subscribe, we think that the great jazz trumpeter Louis Armstrong had things just about right, when he said:

There's only two ways to sum up music: either it's good or it's bad. If it's good you don't mess about it – you just enjoy it.

How to use this *Friendly Guide*

This book is intended to give you an overview of classical music's development from its earliest times right through to the present day. There is so much classical music that has been composed over the years that it would be impossible to include all of it in this one slim volume. Instead, we have concentrated here on the main composers that you will hear played regularly on Classic FM. We have added in one or two other composers whose music we play less often, but who have had an important role in the development of classical music.

After the timeline in Chapter 1, which allows you to put each of our great composers into historical context, the next six chapters of the book take you on a journey through the five main eras of classical music: Early, Baroque, Classical, Romantic and the 20th and 21st centuries. You will find handy "At a glance" guides to each of the main composers featured in the book in the grey boxes throughout these six chapters.

The second part of our *Friendly Guide to Music* includes a guide to the CD which you will find on the inside cover of this book, along with advice on how to immerse yourself even further in the world of classical music. We have also included a Mood Chart (page 216), highlighting specific works that you might wish to listen to, depending on how you feel at a particular time on a particular day.

We wanted to make our guide as friendly on the eye as possible, so we have adopted the same style that we have used in the other books in this series:

- titles of all musical works are set in italics
- songs and arias appear in italics within quotation marks
- nicknames for a particular work also appear in italics with quotation marks, usually after the work's formal title.

We hope that you enjoy uncovering the rich tapestry of sounds, emotions and stories, which go together to make up classical music. And, we hope that you will come to share our view that this is truly the greatest music ever written.

XV

The Friendly Guide to Who Was Composing When

This timeline brings together in one place all of the composers featured in our *Friendly Guide*, allowing you to see whose life crossed over with whom. Classical music doesn't exist in isolation, so the fourth column features a list of events that took place around the world in the year of each composer's birth or death.

Don't be confused by where a composer sits in relation to the beginning of each of the eras. In most cases, our composers didn't become well

1

known for their music until adulthood, so you will find that in some instances their lives straddle more than one era. All will become clear on our journey through classical music in the chapters that follow.

YEAR	Who was born?	Who died?	What else was going on in the world?
		Early Music	
1098	Hildegard of Bingen		St Robert founds the first Cistercian monastery at Cîteaux, France
1179		Hildegard of Bingen	Grand Assize of Windsor, increasing the power of the English royal courts
1300	Guillaume de Machaut		Wenceslas II is crowned King of Poland
1377		Guillaume de Machaut	Pope Gregory XI returns to Rome, ending the Babylonian Captivity in Avignon
1390	John Dunstable		Robert III is crowned King of Scotland
1397	Guillaume Dufay		Denmark, Norway and Sweden are united under one crown
1453		John Dunstable	The end of the Hundred Years' War
1474		Guillaume Dufay	German astronomer Regiomontanus describes how to find longitude by using lunar distances
1490	John Taverner		Printing of books on paper becomes more common in Europe
1505	Thomas Tallis		The Portuguese found Mozambique
1525	Giovanni Pierluigi da Palestrina		Battle of Pavia – the Imperialists capture Francis I

CONTINUED ▶

3

YEAR	Who was born?	Who died?	What else was going on in the world?
1540	William Byrd		Henry VIII marries and divorces Anne of Cleves, and then marries Catherine Howard
1545		John Taverner	Pope John III sets out to reform the Catholic Church through the Council of Trent
1561	Jacopo Peri		Mary Queen of Scots returns to Scotland
1567	Claudio Monteverdi		James VI becomes King of Scotland
1582	Gregorio Allegri		Pope Gregory XIII introduces the Gregorian calendar
1583	Orlando Gibbons		First life insurance policy is taken out
1585		Thomas Tallis	English troops involved in the Spanish–Dutch war
1594		Giovanni Pierluigi da Palestrina	Henri IV is crowned King of France
			The Baroque Period
1600			
1623		William Byrd	The Dutch massacre the English at Amboina in the Moluccas Islands
1625		Orlando Gibbons	Charles I becomes King of England
1632	Jean-Baptiste Lully		The Swedes win the Battle of Lützen, but Gustavus Adolphus II is killed
1633		Jacopo Peri	William Laud becomes Archbishop of Canterbury

YEAR	Who was born?	Who died?	What else was going on in the world?
1643	Marc-Antoine Charpentier	Claudio Monteverdi	Louis XIV is crowned King of France at the age of just five
1652		Gregorio Allegri	The first Anglo–Dutch war begins
1653	Arcangelo Corelli Johann Pachelbel		Oliver Cromwell becomes the Lord Protector of England
1659	Henry Purcell		France replaces Spain as the European superpower
1671	Tomaso Giovanni Albinoni		Uprisings by peasants and Cossacks in Russia come to an end
1678	Antonio Vivaldi		Titus Oates wrongly claims that Catholics have been plotting to murder Charles II
1681	Georg Philipp Telemann		Charles II begins to rule without parliament
1685	Domenico Scarlatti George Frideric Handel Johann Sebastian Bach		James II is crowned King of England – in Scotland he is James VII
1687		Jean-Baptiste Lully	James II of England extends toleration to all religions
1688	Domenico Zipoli		England's "Glorious Revolution"

CONTINUED ▶

5

YEAR	Who was born?	Who died?	What else was going on in the world?
1695		Henry Purcell	The freedom of the press is established in England
1704		Marc-Antoine Charpentier	Duke of Marlborough defeats France at Battle of Blenheim
1706		Johann Pachelbel	Duke of Marlborough defeats France at Battle of Ramillies
1713		Arcangelo Corelli	Treaty of Utrecht ends War of Spanish Succession
1714	Christoph Willibald von Gluck Carl Philippe Emanuel Bach		George I is crowned King of Great Britain and Ireland
1726		Domenico Zipoli	Cardinal Fleury becomes chief minister in France
1732	Franz Joseph Haydn		George Washington is born
1735	Johann Christian Bach		War of Polish Succession ends
1739	Karl Ditters von Dittersdorf		War of Jenkins' Ear between Britain and Spain
1741		Antonio Vivaldi	Sweden and Russia at war
1743	Luigi Boccherini		George II leads British army to victory over French at Dettingen

YEAR	Who was born?	Who died?	What else was going on in the world?
1750			**The Classical Period**
	Antonio Salieri	Tomaso Giovanni Albinoni	Minor earthquake in London
		Johann Sebastian Bach	
1756	Wolfgang Amadeus Mozart		Seven Years' War begins
1757		Domenico Scarlatti	Clive conquers Bengal
1759		George Frideric Handel	James Brindley designs Worsley–Manchester Canal
1767		Georg Philipp Telemann	James Cook sets out on the voyage that will see the discovery of Australia
1770	Ludwig van Beethoven		James Cook discovers "New South Wales"
1782	Niccolò Paganini	Johann Christian Bach	Rodney victorious at Battle of the Saints, saving British West Indies
1784	Louis Spohr		Samuel Johnson dies
1786	Carl Maria von Weber		Commercially made ice cream first advertised in New York
1787		Christoph Willibald von Gluck	American Constitution drafted and signed at Philadelphia

CONTINUED ▶

YEAR	Who was born?	Who died?	What else was going on in the world?
1788		Carl Philippe Emanuel Bach	The first British convicts are transported to Australia
1791		Wolfgang Amadeus Mozart	Louis XVI and Marie Antoinette flee
1792	Gioacchino Rossini		France becomes a Republic
1797	Franz Schubert		Napoleon forces Austria to make peace with France
1799		Karl Ditters von Dittersdorf	Egyptian hieroglyphics understood through the discovery of the Rosetta Stone
1803	Hector Berlioz		France sells Louisiana to the USA
1804	Johann Strauss Sr Mikhail Glinka		Spain declares war on Britain
1805		Luigi Boccherini	Nelson is victorious at Battle of Trafalgar
1809	Felix Mendelssohn	Franz Joseph Haydn	British are defeated at Battle of Corunna
1810	Frédéric Chopin Robert Schumann		Argentina becomes independent from Spain
1811	Franz Liszt		George III of England is declared insane

YEAR	Who was born?	Who died?	What else was going on in the world?
1813	Giuseppe Verdi Richard Wagner		Allied forces invade France
1819	Jacques Offenbach		Singapore is founded
1824	Anton Bruckner Bedřich Smetana		Trades unions legalized in Britain
1825	Johann Strauss Jr	Antonio Salieri	First railway opens from Stockton to Darlington
1826		Carl Maria von Weber	Menai suspension bridge opens
1827		Ludwig van Beethoven	Treaty of London guarantees Greek independence
1828		Franz Schubert	Russia and Turkey at war
1830			**The Romantic Period**
1833	Johannes Brahms Alexander Borodin		Factory Act prevents children under nine from working in factories
1835	Camille Saint-Saëns		The word "socialism" first used
1836	Léo Délibes		Texas is granted independence from Mexico
1838	Georges Bizet Max Bruch		National Gallery moves to London's Trafalgar Square

CONTINUED ▶

YEAR	Who was born?	Who died?	What else was going on in the world?
1839	Modest Mussorgsky		Britain and Afghanistan at war
1840	Pyotr Ilyich Tchaikovsky	Niccolò Paganini	Penny postage is introduced in Britain
1841	Antonín Dvořák		Britain acquires Hong Kong
1842	Arthur Sullivan		Irish potato famine begins
1843	Edvard Grieg		Natal becomes a British colony
1844	Nikolai Rimsky-Korsakov		First message is sent in Morse code
1845	Gabriel Fauré		Texas joins the USA
1847		Felix Mendelssohn	The British Museum opens
1849		Johann Strauss Sr Frédéric Chopin	Punjab is annexed by Britain
1856		Robert Schumann	Livingstone completes journey across Africa
1857	Edward Elgar	Mikhail Glinka	Indian Mutiny
1858	Giacomo Puccini		Great Eastern is launched
1859		Louis Spohr	Darwin publishes Origin of Species
1860	Gustav Mahler Isaac Albéniz		Anglo-Chinese War ends

YEAR	Who was born?	Who died?	What else was going on in the world?
1862	Frederick Delius Claude Debussy		Cotton famine in Lancashire
1864	Richard Strauss		Karl Marx founds *First International* in London
1865	Jean Sibelius		William Booth founds Salvation Army
1866	Erik Satie		Austro-Prussian war ends
1868		Gioacchino Rossini	Disraeli becomes prime minister in Britain but is defeated by Gladstone in election
1869			Suez Canal formally opens
1872	Ralph Vaughan Williams	Hector Berlioz	Secret ballot is introduced in Britain
1873	Sergei Rachmaninov		Spain becomes a republic
1874	Gustav Holst Arnold Schoenberg		Spain stops being a republic
1875	Maurice Ravel	Georges Bizet	Britain buys shares in Suez Canal
1880		Jacques Offenbach	Boer revolt against British in South Africa
1881	Béla Bartók	Modest Mussorgsky	Pasteur proves animals can be immunized against anthrax
1882	Igor Stravinsky		Cairo is occupied by British troops

CONTINUED ▶

11

YEAR	Who was born?	Who died?	What else was going on in the world?
1883		Richard Wagner	Germany introduces National Insurance
1884		Bedřich Smetana	Greenwich meridian is recognized as prime meridian
1886		Franz Liszt	Daimler produces his first motor car
1887		Alexander Borodin	Queen Victoria celebrates jubilee
1891	Sergei Prokofiev	Léo Délibes	United States of Brazil created
1893		Pyotr Ilyich Tchaikovsky	Irish Home Rule Bill defeated by House of Lords
1896		Anton Bruckner	Gold discovered in the Klondike
1897		Johannes Brahms	Great Gold Rush begins
1898	George Gershwin		The Curies discover radium
1899	Francis Poulenc	Johann Strauss Jr	Boer War begins
1900	Aaron Copland	Arthur Sullivan	Australian Commonwealth is proclaimed
1901	Joaquín Rodrigo	Giuseppe Verdi	Trans-Siberian railway opens
1902	William Walton		Boer War ends
1904		Antonín Dvořák	*Entente cordiale* between Britain and France
1906	Dmitri Shostakovich		Vitamins discovered by F. G. Hopkins

YEAR	Who was born?	Who died?	What else was going on in the world?
1907		Edvard Grieg	*Entente cordiale* between Britain and Russia
1908		Nikolai Rimsky-Korsakov	Asquith becomes British prime minister
1909		Isaac Albéniz	Henry Ford begins "assembly line" production of cars
1910			**The Era of 20th and 21st Century Composers**
1910	Samuel Barber		Tolstoy and Florence Nightingale die
1911		Gustav Mahler	National Insurance is introduced in Britain
1912			*Titanic* sinks
1913	John Cage		Third Irish Home Rule Bill passes House of Commons
1918	Benjamin Britten	Claude Debussy	Women over 30 get the vote in Britain
1920	Leonard Bernstein	Max Bruch	Degrees first open to women at Oxford University
1921		Camille Saint-Saëns	Irish Free State is established
1924		Giacomo Puccini Gabriel Fauré	First Labour government in Britain
1925		Erik Satie	Summer Time Act made permanent
1932	John Williams		Sydney Harbour Bridge opens
1933	Henryk Górecki John Barry		Prohibition ends in USA

CONTINUED ▶

YEAR	Who was born?	Who died?	What else was going on in the world?
1934	Peter Maxwell Davies	Edward Elgar Frederick Delius Gustav Holst	Hitler becomes German dictator
1935	Arvo Pärt		Hitler announces rearmament of German forces
1937	Philip Glass	Maurice Ravel George Gershwin	British coalition government formed under Neville Chamberlain
1942	Paul McCartney		First controlled nuclear chain reaction in uranium
1943		Sergei Rachmaninov	German forces at Stalingrad surrender
1944	John Tavener Karl Jenkins		First V-2 falls on England
1945	John Rutter	Béla Bartók	World War Two ends
1946	Howard Shore		Americans test atom bomb at Bikini
1949		Richard Strauss	Chairman Mao Tse-tung proclaims People's Republic of China
1951		Arnold Schoenberg	Sir Winston Churchill becomes British prime minister for the second time
1953	James Horner	Sergei Prokofiev	Hilary and Tensing climb Everest
1955	Ludovico Einaudi		Sir Winston Churchill resigns, to be replaced by Sir Anthony Eden
1957	Hans Zimmer	Jean Sibelius	UK's first hydrogen bomb test

YEAR	Who was born?	Who died?	What else was going on in the world?
1958	Patrick Hawes	Ralph Vaughan Williams	Gatwick airport opens
1963		Francis Poulenc	£2.6m stolen in British "Great Train Robbery"
1971	Joby Talbot	Igor Stravinsky	British Education secretary Mrs Thatcher announces end of free school milk
1975		Dmitri Shostakovich	UK votes in referendum to join the European Community
1976		Benjamin Britten	James Callaghan becomes British prime minister
1981		Samuel Barber	President Reagan shot in Washington
1983		William Walton	First UK heart-lung transplant
1990		Aaron Copland Leonard Bernstein	Nelson Mandela is freed after 25 years in jail
1992		John Cage	Classic FM begins broadcasting
1999		Joaquín Rodrigo	Yehudi Menuhin dies

02

Early Music

In the beginning

Music has been around for a long time. Historians have no doubt about that, although there are differing opinions about exactly when and where the idea of making musical instruments to play tunes first took hold. Fragments of primitive instruments which were crafted more than ten centuries ago have been found by archaeologists in places as far apart as Germany, Spain, Egypt and China.

Human beings are inherently musical. We can make all sorts of sounds with just our bodies, and the earliest musicians probably had no need for instrumental add-ons at all. Singing, clapping and even foot tapping are all forms of music. In fact, they are used today as a means of teaching very young children about the rudiments of making music.

When we talk about **Early Music** in the classical music world, we have a fairly clear idea about what we mean. It's not necessarily the earliest music known to humankind. Instead, the term tends to be used to describe the earliest forms of Western classical music, principally being composed between 1000 and 1600, covering the **Medieval** and **Renaissance** periods.

What else was going on in the world?

Well, in the year 1000, the Viking Biarni Heriulfsson was blown off course and sighted the coast of America. The continent was not actually discovered officially by a European for almost another 500 years, when Christopher Columbus landed in the West Indies in 1492.

The dawning of the second millennium saw England under attack from the Danes. In 1012, the invading forces rampaged through Canterbury, although they were bought off with 48,000 pounds of silver.

King Canute ruled England from 1017 to 1035 and King Harold was briefly on the throne in 1066 until William the Conqueror took over the crown following the Battle of Hastings. Scotland's kings included Macbeth from 1040 to 1057.

In fact, what we consider now to be **Early Music** was composed right through the time that England was reigned over by members of the House of Plantagenet (1154–1399), the House of Lancaster (1399–1461), the House of York (1461–1485) and the House of Tudor, ending with the reign of Elizabeth I between 1558 and 1603. In Scotland, James VI was on the throne from 1567, becoming James I of England following Elizabeth I's death in 1603.

This period encompasses the Crusades, the signing of the Magna Carta, the devastating scourge of the Black Death across Europe and the Hundred Years' War between Britain and France, from 1337 to 1453.

So, the world was a busy place, with warfare at the top of many people's agendas as one tribe or nation plotted to take over another, only to find their efforts reversed a few years later. However, as you will see, there were huge developments in music, many of which were brought about by the Catholic Church.

Ambrose and Gregory

Although the title above sounds like a 1970s television sitcom, Ambrose was in fact Bishop of Milan between 374 and 397; and Gregory I was Pope between 590 and 604. Among the latter's many claims to fame was his decision to send Augustine to England to convert the locals to Christianity.

Bishop Ambrose and Pope Gregory are generally credited with making great strides in the evolution of **plainsong**, which was the unaccompanied singing that took place as part of church services, most often performed by monks.

Ambrose was an important figure in the development of **antiphonal** singing, where two parts of a choir sing alternately, with the second section answering the first. Gregory's contribution is, however, more often remembered by musical historians, and he is given the credit for a more general overhaul of this area of music a couple of hundred years later. He gave his name to the result, and Gregorian Chant was born.

You can hear an example of Gregorian Chant on **CD Track 1**. See page 187 for more information.

19

Hitting the right note

People had been trying to write down music for a while by the 1000s, but there was no truly uniform method for making a record of exactly who had to sing what note when, and for how long.

We know that instrumental music was also being made in the centuries before the end of the first millennium, but there is no accurate record of what sort of tunes were being composed, so we can only imagine how they might have sounded.

In around 1025, a monk called Guido d'Arezzo published his theories on musical notation. He had developed a system which meant that chants could be read and then sung by anyone who had learnt to decipher the code that he had created. Today, we call this deciphering "reading music".

For this reason, we are able to understand and give authentic performances of music written 1000 years ago. It means that the heritage of classical music has been preserved in a way that other musical genres from around the world simply have not been. We have a lot to thank Guido d'Arezzo for.

The really early composers

The first composer in our *Friendly Guide to Music* is a woman. She is, in fact, the only female composer

featured with anything other than a walk-on part in the whole of this book. If you read through the list of the Top 100 works in the Classic FM Hall of Fame on pages 199–203, you will notice that no pieces by women feature among our listeners' favourites and there are actually none in the next 200 most popular either.

At a glance: Hildegard of Bingen

Born: 1098
Died: 1179
Nationality: German
Must listen: *A Feather on the Breath of God*

You can hear an example of Hildegard's music on **CD Track 2**. See page 187 for more information.

But that does nothing to take away from the achievements of **Hildegard of Bingen**. Although she was born into a noble family in 1098, she was sent away to a monastery at the age of just eight. By the time she was 38, she had become the leader of the nuns who were based at the monastery, and around 12 years later, she founded her own nunnery near the town of Bingen.

Hildegard was no ordinary nun. Apart from having a gift for writing poetry and music, she became an influential diplomat, corresponding regularly with religious and secular leaders. As a thinker, she

made her name in areas such as science and medicine.

Hildegard became famed as a mystic, and between 1141 and 1170, she had no fewer than 26 visions. She wrote down their details and set them to music.

People travelled from far and wide to consult Hildegard, and when she died at the age of 81 (a remarkable achievement in itself at the time), the Catholic Church considered making her a saint, although she was never actually canonized.

At a glance: Guillaume de Machaut

Born: Around 1300
Died: 1377
Nationality: French
Must listen: *Messe de Notre Dame* – his famous four-part mass

Some composers lived for the moment and others spent their time worrying about their legacy. **Guillaume de Machaut** was firmly in the latter camp, although he was not without talent: he counted Geoffrey Chaucer among his fans. Machaut was one of the "Ars Nova" composers who were responsible for many innovations in French and Italian classical music during the 1300s. In particular, he is remembered for developing new ways of using rhythms.

Machaut became a canon in Rheims when he was about 40, and he seems to have spent much of the rest of his life bossing around the monks who were instructed to reproduce copies of his complete works. His desire for musical immortality was not in vain and he is one of the best-known composers of the period, simply because so much of his music still survives.

Although he was a priest, this doesn't seem to have stopped Machaut writing extensively on the subject of unfulfilled passion, and many of his songs were not religious at all. Instead, he adopted the style of the troubadours, wandering poets and musicians who performed their work in the homes of the French nobility.

However, it's for his four-part mass that Machaut is most respected. He was among the first composers to write four separate tunes for people with different voices which combined together harmoniously, and this was a big step forward in the history of classical music. This new style of singing was known as **polyphony**.

The Renaissance men

As you will discover as our story unfolds, there are periods in the history of classical music where similar developments occurred simultaneously in different countries.

One of the big times of change in the type of classical music that was written was what we now call the **Renaissance Period**. Literally translated from the French, this means "re-birth". The British tend to think of **John Dunstable** as heading up their group (or "school") of Renaissance composers, while in France, it was the Belgian **Guillaume Dufay** who was carrying the torch for the re-birth.

At a glance: John Dunstable

Born: Around 1390
Died: 1453
Nationality: English
Must listen: *Preco Preheminencie*

The Renaissance was not just going on in the world of music; the new discoveries also spanned science, exploration and the visual arts.

John Dunstable was one of English music's greatest exports and, rather like The Beatles in the 1960s, he was very much the face of English music abroad in the mid 1400s. Composers around Europe were impressed by his style of writing, and incorporated many of his new ideas into their own compositions. All of this popularity led to Dunstable becoming something of a property magnate back home, with a string of houses to his name across the south of England.

Almost all of the music Dunstable wrote was for use in the church, and he managed to create a particularly rich sound. Guillaume Dufay was one of the continental composers who was influenced by Dunstable's music.

At a glance: Guillaume Dufay

Born: Around 1397
Died: 1474
Nationality: Belgian
Must listen: *Mass "L'Homme Armé"*

Dufay was the illegitimate son of a priest, who began his musical career as a boy chorister at Cambrai Cathedral. He moved on to Bologna in Italy and worked for the Pope in Rome and Florence. In the 1450s, Dufay composed a mass based on a folk song called "*L'Homme Armé*", which translates as "The armed man". He was one of a long line of composers in musical history to use this title for a mass – the most recent of whom is the Welshman Karl Jenkins, whose *The Armed Man (A Mass for Peace)* was premiered in 2000.

Dufay wrote every sort of music that had been invented at the time, including a wide variety of religious music and a range of secular songs. Word has it that he was also the first composer to write a requiem mass, but this is hard to prove definitively because the manuscript has been lost in the passage of time.

At a glance: John Taverner

Born:	Around 1490
Died:	1545
Nationality:	English
Must listen:	*Mass "The Western Wynde"* for four voices

Now, it's easy to become confused about our next composer, **John Taverner**. Don't mistake him for John Tavener (without the extra "r"), who is alive and well and composing music as you read this. We will come to him much later on in Chapter 7 of our *Friendly Guide*.

John Taverner was one of the big stars of English music in this period. As well as being a composer, he was a friend of Thomas Cromwell, one of the main forces behind the dissolution of the monasteries. It is possible that Taverner was a supporter of these reforms – he is on record as saying that he was embarrassed to have composed "popish ditties" early on in his career as a composer. This idea is explored in a 1970 opera called *Taverner*, which was written by Sir Peter Maxwell Davies who is now the Master of the Queen's Music. Again, more on him much later on in this book (see Chapter 7).

Thomas Tallis was another mighty force in English music. He was composing throughout the reigns of Henry VIII, who broke away from Rome and created the Church of England; Edward VI; Mary I;

At a glance: Thomas Tallis

Born: Around 1505
Died: 1585
Nationality: English
Must listen: *Spem in Alium*

who was a Catholic; and Elizabeth I, who was a Protestant. Considering that Tallis managed to write music for the church during all four of these reigns, he must have been as good at bending his style to suit the prevailing wind as he was at composing the music in the first place.

Tallis's exact provenance has been lost in the mists of time, but he was probably brought up near Canterbury, working first as an organist at Dover Priory. He then moved to Waltham Abbey in Essex in the same role, before becoming a lay clerk at Canterbury Cathedral.

From 1543 until his death more than four decades later, Tallis operated a job share with his pupil **William Byrd** as the composer and organist to the Chapel Royal.

William Byrd was known as "the father of British music". The fact that he survived to write anything at all is surprising, considering that he was known to be a Catholic supporter at a time when this was

At a glance: William Byrd

Born: Around 1540
Died: 1623
Nationality: English
Must listen: *Ave Verum Corpus*

punishable by death. He became organist and
choirmaster at Lincoln Cathedral in 1563, where he
stayed until 1572 when he moved to London to
take up the job share with Thomas Tallis.

Whereas Tallis only wrote a few pieces that were not
for the church, Byrd left behind some excellent
examples of keyboard music and of madrigals,
which were unaccompanied songs for a group of
voices.

Byrd and Tallis lived out their lives in relative
financial comfort because of the beneficence of
Elizabeth I. She granted them jointly a patent that
allowed them a complete monopoly on printing
music and music paper in England for 21 years
from 1575. Their first publication was called
Cantiones Sacrae, which translates as "Sacred Songs".
It was made up of a total of 34 different songs – 17
by each composer.

This new means of distributing music meant that,
for the first time, choirs could sing music from
printed sheets, making it far easier for musical

works to become established right across the country.

At a glance: Giovanni Pierluigi da Palestrina

Born: Around 1525
Died: 1594
Nationality: Italian
Must listen: *Missa Papae Marcelli*

You can hear an excerpt from this mass on **CD Track 3**. See page 188 for more information.

Back to Italy now, and it is important to remember that innovation in sacred music was not necessarily welcomed with open arms by the Catholic Church. Some of the changes were even the subject of papal decrees. With the rise of Protestantism, any modification of the status quo tended to be regarded as an all-out attack on the foundations of the church itself. Some senior members of the church even advocated changing things back to the style written by composers of the likes of Hildegard of Bingen, because they believed that the fancy new way of writing music meant that the sacred texts no longer had the same powerful meaning.

Giovanni Pierluigi da Palestrina was asked to compose a mass that would definitively prove one

way or another whether polyphony really was the way forward for church music, rather than the plainsong of old.

Palestrina produced a mass that was so beautiful that the critics gave up and the polyphonic brigade was victorious. He dedicated his new piece, which was composed around 1561, to Pope Marcellus. The Pope only reigned for 55 days and never actually heard the music that was written especially for him.

Palestrina had some particularly unhappy periods during his life. In the 1570s, his family was torn apart by the plague, which was sweeping through Europe with devastating consequences. His wife, brother and two of his sons all succumbed to the terrible disease.

We now stay in Italy for the rest of this period of classical music. As you will see as our *Friendly Guide* continues, there were strong English, French, Austrian, German, Russian and Eastern European influences on classical music at various times in its history. Italy could argue the case for being the most influential country of all – and nowhere has that Italian influence been more keenly felt than in the world of opera.

Opera is the plural of the Latin word *opus*, meaning "work", and it was a really major development in classical music. In its most basic form, opera marks

At a glance: Jacopo Peri

Born: 1561
Died: 1633
Nationality: Italian
Must listen: The oldest remaining opera *Euridice*

the coming together of words and music in an equal partnership.

The man to whom history has given the credit for writing the world's first opera is one **Jacopo Peri**, whose first operatic work was *Dafne*. The composer himself was something of a performer and he took the role of Apollo in the first production in 1598. Although we know the opera performance took place, the music has now been lost. However, Peri's second opera, *Euridice*, does still exist and is occasionally performed today.

At a glance: Claudio Monteverdi

Born: 1567
Died: 1643
Nationality: Italian
Must listen: *Vespers for the Blessed Virgin*

Although he has no right to claim the title at all, many people consider **Claudio Monteverdi**'s *La Favola d'Orfeo* to be the first true opera. It's based on the same story as *Euridice* and, in fact, Orpheus

(Orfeo) and Euridice are husband and wife in the mythological tale. The story goes that Orpheus was so distraught at Euridice's death that he visited Hades, the land of the dead, to try to get her back. He ultimately fails in his quest. It was a story to which other composers returned time and time again during later periods of classical music.

Monteverdi is also known today for his sacred music, and in particular for his *Vespers for the Blessed Virgin*, which were dedicated to Pope Paul V. This is a strikingly beautiful piece of music which was written shortly after both Monteverdi's wife and only child had died. It is quite likely that his own personal suffering is mirrored in the music.

The end of early music

The advent of opera marks the end of the longest period of music in our *Friendly Guide*, beginning at the dawn of time, or around the year 1000, depending on your point of view, and ending at around the turn of the 17th century.

It is worth noting at this point that the beginning and end of each musical era cannot be pinpointed to an absolute moment in time. One set of composers did not simply stop writing, to be replaced by a new team waiting patiently on the subs bench. Instead, new styles of music gradually replaced the old styles – and just as plainsong gave way to polyphony and Medieval composers were replaced by Renaissance composers, so they in turn faded away. You will be relieved to know that our story most certainly doesn't end there, though.

The Baroque Period

Baroque 'n' roll

Had this book been written by an American, the heading above would probably have been "If it ain't baroque, don't fix it", because our cousins across the Atlantic pronounce the word "Baroque" with a long "o", so the second syllable rhymes with "poke". But back here in Britain, we always pronounce it with a short "o", to rhyme with "clock".

Anyway, enough of the pronunciation guide. We are now in the period of classical music that runs from 1600 to 1750. This was a rather exciting time in history, with plenty of storylines for action movies: Guy Fawkes attempted to blow up the Houses of Parliament in the Gunpowder Plot; the Pilgrim Fathers set sail on the Mayflower from Plymouth for a new life in America; and Charles I was beheaded. It was also a period of enormous scientific advancement: Isaac Newton realized that the earth had a gravitational pull, so the story goes, after being hit on the head by an apple; and astronomers also decided once and for all that the earth orbits the sun, rather than vice versa.

From Church to nobility

The Church was still an important force in deciding what music would be written, not least because it employed so many composers in a variety of musical positions. However, as the story of the **Baroque period** unfurls, you will begin to notice a shift in power. Gradually, the Church becomes a less important force in the commissioning of new music, to be replaced by the nobility, who listened to music chiefly for recreational pleasure rather than out of devotional duty, and who commissioned composers and employed musicians as a means of showing off their status within society.

We begin our journey through the Baroque composers with two men who are firmly in the sacred music camp.

At a glance: Gregorio Allegri

Born: 1582
Died: 1652
Nationality: Italian
Must listen: *Miserere*

Gregorio Allegri was steeped in the traditions of the Catholic Church, becoming a choirboy at the age of nine and ending up as music director of the papal choir two years before his death.

He is best known today for his *Miserere*, which was performed every year during Holy Week from the time it was written until towards the end of the 19th century. The Vatican kept the lid on the exact details of what was being sung, and anyone who made an illegal copy of the music was threatened with severe punishment. The *Miserere* was probably even more stunning to listen to back in Allegri's time than it is today because the members of the highly skilled papal choir would add their own embellishments to the music – an example of 17th-century choral jamming, if you like. This piece of music also warrants a mention during the life of one Wolfgang Amadeus Mozart in Chapter 4 of our *Friendly Guide*.

The English Composer **Orlando Gibbons** was a member of the Chapel Royal. This choir still exists today and is an important part of the royal

At a glance: Orlando Gibbons

Born: 1583
Died: 1625
Nationality: English
Must listen: *This is the Record of John*

household's music-making. You will often see the choir performing at state occasions. The Chapel Royal was something of a hothouse for the best musical talent in England and, because it was the monarch's own choir, it was able to cherry-pick the very best musicians from all of the other choirs around the country. As well as Orlando Gibbons, Thomas Tallis, William Byrd and Henry Purcell were all important members of this august body.

Gibbons was a particularly talented organist, and he also wrote keyboard works and pieces to be performed by consorts (groups of musicians). It is worth noting that Gibbons was the first major composer to write exclusively for the Anglican church. He died tragically young while with the royal household in Canterbury, where he is buried in the Cathedral.

Jean-Baptiste Lully held a privileged position in the French court, working as the personal composer to King Louis XIV. His job made him the most important man in French music, and for more than

At a glance: Jean-Baptiste Lully

Born: 1632
Died: 1687
Nationality: Initially Italian, then French
Must listen: The ballet music that he wrote for King
             Louis XIV

two decades he was able to exert enormous control over the country's musical life.

During this time, Lully achieved a lot, particularly in developing the sound of the orchestra. After his changes, the orchestra looked and sounded far closer to the ones we have today than they did to those that had pre-dated him.

Lully was undoubtedly an innovator and a visionary. Many of the instruments that he brought into the orchestra had only just been invented, so, although an orchestra made up of 24 violins, plus flutes, oboes, bassoons, trumpets and timpani might seem normal to us, it was absolutely revolutionary in the 1600s.

Lully also bought the right to be the only man in France to be allowed to put on operas – he staged his first production on a converted tennis court. He was also extremely influential in the area of music publishing and became well known for writing ballets.

Lully's death was the stuff of legend. Rather than the conductor's baton that we know today, Lully used a long stick to beat time on the floor when he was conducting his orchestra. One day, he missed the floor and speared his own foot instead. Gangrene set in and he died two months later after refusing to have his foot amputated. His royal patronage did, however, ensure that he died an extremely rich man.

At a glance: Marc-Antoine Charpentier

Born:	1643
Died:	1704
Nationality:	*French*
Must listen:	*Te Deum*

Although he lived at the same time as Lully, **Marc-Antoine Charpentier** was never part of Louis XIV's court. His choral music has come back into fashion in recent years, but his best-known work is infamous for an altogether different reason.

Next time you settle down in front of the television to watch the Eurovision Song Contest, listen to the opening theme music; it is the trumpet tune at the very start of Charpentier's *Te Deum* that is played. You can rest assured that it will be just about the only piece of music that you hear all evening that doesn't deserve "nul points".

At a glance: Arcangelo Corelli

Born: 1653
Died: 1713
Nationality: Italian
Must listen: *Concerto Grosso Op. 6 No.8*, known as *The Christmas Concerto*

Arcangelo Corelli was born into a rich family and was lucky enough not to face the hand-to-mouth financial struggles that many other composers were forced to endure. Despite what some of the self-appointed grandees of the classical music world would have you believe, most composers tended to write music as a means of putting food on their tables, a roof over their heads and clothes on their backs, and not because of some sort of flight of artistic fancy.

Perhaps it was Corelli's relative wealth that made him less hungry to produce a copious amount of work, or perhaps, because he didn't need to keep an eye on the money coming in, he could spend more time refining his music, but he was by no means the most prolific composer of his time. He was, however, celebrated across Europe, and many of the greatest composers who followed him, such as Bach and Handel, were undoubtedly influenced by the music he wrote.

Corelli was an outstanding violin player, and he is the first of our featured composers to make their name purely from the composition of instrumental music. He also brought some new thinking to the way that orchestras performed, insisting that all the string players mirrored each other's playing style by moving their bows up and down in the same direction at the same time. Believe it or not, this actually changed the sound made by the orchestra, allowing the musicians to give a more precise performance. It also made Corelli's orchestras far more aesthetically pleasing, and his concerts became popular because they were as easy on the eye as they were on the ear.

Corelli was also the master of the "Concerto Grosso", a type of musical work where the orchestra is divided into two different groups. A group of musicians tended to play first, with a second group then echoing the music played by the first set. This created a sense of drama between loud and soft parts of the music and the two groups of players.

At a glance: Johann Pachelbel

Born: 1653
Died: 1706
Nationality: German
Must listen: *Canon in D*

At Classic FM, we have a term for those composers who are known for one great work that dwarfs all of the rest of their output. We call them "one-hit wonders". The German **Johann Pachelbel** is a prime example of the species, with his *Canon in D* a firm favourite in all sorts of environments, not least as an accompaniment to the walk down the aisle at many weddings.

Many composers wrote canons – but nobody else achieved quite the same fame for it. It's a simple idea in which a melody is played and then imitated by one or more other instruments. You may unwittingly have performed a canon yourself as a child when you sang *"Frère Jacques", "Three Blind Mice"* or *"London's Burning"*. In these cases, the canon is sometimes referred to as a *round*.

Although the *Canon in D* is pretty much all he is remembered for now, Pachelbel was massive in the world of keyboard and chamber music in the late 17th century. By the way, any piece that is written for small groups of musicians to play counts as chamber music. We even have chamber orchestras, which are smaller than symphony orchestras and often feature up to around 30 players.

This book is filled to the brim with musical prodigies and **Henry Purcell** is the first of them. It is just as well that his talent was identified and nurtured while he was young, because he was just 36 years old when

At a glance: Henry Purcell

Born: 1659
Died: 1695
Nationality: English
Must listen: *"When I Am Laid in Earth"* (known as
                 "Dido's Lament"); the *Rondo* from *Abdelazer*;
                 Trumpet Tune and Air in D; *Come Ye Sons
                 of Art*

 You can hear an excerpt from *"Dido's Lament"* on
CD Track 4. See page 188 for more information.

he died – although he achieved more than many
composers who live to be twice his age. Music
historians say that his death was a real set-back for the
development of English music. It was not for another
200 years that England would produce another truly
great composer, in the shape of Edward Elgar.

By the time Purcell was ten, he was one of the
Children of the Chapel Royal (a choirboy). Just a
decade later, he was given one of the most
prestigious musical jobs of the moment when he
was made organist of Westminster Abbey.

Purcell produced a large amount of music,
considering his short life, and its range was wide –
taking in organ solos, sacred anthems, secular songs,
chamber music and music to be performed in the
theatre. He wrote works for Charles II, James II and
Queen Mary.

Purcell's only opera, *Dido and Aeneas*, tells the story of Dido, the Queen of Carthage. She is in love with Aeneas, who has sailed away to found Rome. She is devastated and sings the haunting aria *"When I Am Laid in Earth"* – in our opinion the greatest thing Purcell ever wrote.

At a glance: Tomaso Giovanni Albinoni

Born:	1671
Died:	Around 1750
Nationality:	Italian
Must listen:	*Adagio in G minor, Oboe Concerto No. 2*

Our next composer is most famous for a piece of music that he never actually completed. The music that we today regard as being **Tomaso Albinoni**'s *Adagio in G minor* was in fact based on only a fragment of manuscript, rather than a fully defined work. This fragment was taken by an Italian professor, Remo Giazotto, who built it up into the piece we know and love today, based on his studies of the composer's other works. It would be fair to say that Giazotto took an informed guess as to how Albinoni intended the *Adagio* to turn out.

It's hard not to feel just a little sorry for Albinoni because there are plenty of other surviving pieces that he definitely did write, for which he could be remembered. The 300 or so works to his name include more than 50 operas and more than 50 concertos.

At a glance: Antonio Vivaldi

Born: 1678
Died: 1741
Nationality: Italian
Must listen: *Four Seasons; Gloria;* "*Nulla in Mundo Pax Sincera*", which was used in the film *Shine*

You can hear an excerpt from the *Four Seasons* on **CD Track 5**. See page 189 for more information.

Antonio Vivaldi was responsible for what many people reckon is the most recorded piece of classical music of all time: the *Four Seasons*. Every year, new versions are released, but for our money, it's hard to beat the 1989 version by Nigel Kennedy on the EMI Classics label.

It's all the more remarkable that this work has achieved the success it has when you consider that Vivaldi's music was hardly played at all from his death in 1741 right through until the middle of the 20th century. This is all down to a rather strange decision by a nobleman called Count Giacomo Durazzo. He pulled together all of Vivaldi's original works and simply locked them up. In his last will and testament, Durazzo ordered his family to make sure that none of this music by Vivaldi should ever be performed or published. After many years, these

ludicrous instructions were overturned and Vivaldi's music was once more heard. The public lapped up his catchy melodies, and a star was re-born, some 200 years after his death.

Vivaldi certainly rattled out the concertos, with more than 500 of them to his name. Unkind critics suggest that he actually wrote the same tune in a slightly different way 500 times, but we don't think that's entirely fair.

There is no doubt that Vivaldi was a bit of a character. He chose to follow in his father's footsteps and learned to play the violin. He played the instrument while undertaking his religious training, becoming known as "The Red Priest" because of his bright red hair.

Vivaldi was excused having to say Mass because he claimed to suffer from asthma. This illness certainly didn't stop him from conducting or from travelling all over Europe. It also didn't prevent him from enjoying a close relationship with at least one of his travelling companions, a young soprano called Anna Girò and her sister Paolina. He was censured for unpriestly conduct in 1737, despite denying that his relationship with the two women was in any way improper.

Any illicit affairs certainly never got in the way of Vivaldi's composing, though. As well as the 500

concertos, he also wrote more than 50 operas, well over 80 sonatas and more than 120 other sacred and secular vocal pieces.

At a glance: Georg Philipp Telemann

Born: 1681

Died: 1767

Nationality: German

Must listen: *Concerto for Trumpet and Strings in D*

Vivaldi was a mere minnow in terms of productivity when compared to our next composer. In the race to write the largest number of pieces **Georg Philipp Telemann** is not only miles ahead of the rest of the Baroque pack, he storms in front of every other composer that we have featured so far – or in the pages still to come – with around 3,700 different works to his name.

Telemann had a keen ear for the prevailing musical fashions and he also made sure that his pieces were heard far and wide. He was one of the first composers to publish his vocal and instrumental music in a magazine format specifically targeted at amateur music-makers.

Although he was considered to be a real star in Germany during his lifetime, history has not judged Telemann so kindly, and his musical contribution has been completely eclipsed by that of our next

two composers – the undoubted kings of the
Baroque period.

At a glance: Johann Sebastian Bach

Born: 1685

Died: 1750

Nationality: German

Must listen: *Brandenburg Concertos*; *Toccata and Fugue in
D Minor*; *St Matthew Passion*; *Goldberg
Variations*

🔊 You can hear an excerpt from the *Brandenburg
Concertos* on **CD Track 7**. See page 190 for more
information.

George Frideric Handel and **Johann Sebastian
Bach** were born in Germany in the same year. 1685
was a very fine musical vintage indeed.

Johann Sebastian Bach had music in his blood. He
was part of a German musical dynasty that spanned
many generations, both before and after him. Some
people believe that his music actually eclipses that of
those two other giants of the classical music world –
Mozart and Beethoven. Whatever the ranking, there
is no doubt that Bach deserves to be among those
considered as the greatest ever classical composers.

While he was alive, Bach was best known as an
organist, although he was modest about his
achievements in this area:

There's really nothing remarkable about it. All you have to do is hit the right key at the right time and the instrument plays itself.

After he had died, there was a general reassessment of just how good a composer Bach really was and he gained the recognition that he deserved as a master of musical composition, particularly in the areas of choral, keyboard and instrumental works. There is a particularly strong spirituality to his music, which was influenced by Bach's dedicated religious faith.

By the time Johann Sebastian had reached double figures, both of his parents had died. The young boy was sent to live with his older brother, Johann Christoph, who was, like their father, an organist.

Johann Christoph passed his skills on the organ to his younger brother. When Johann Sebastian was 15, he went away to a school 200 miles away and continued to study for another two years.

After leaving school, Johann Sebastian worked as a violinist, before eventually taking up the family business and becoming an organist. One of the best-known stories about Bach concerns the lengths to which he would go to learn more about making music. On one occasion, when he was just 19, he made a 450-mile round trip on foot to hear a concert by his hero, the organist Dietrich Buxtehude.

In 1707, Bach married his cousin, Maria Barbara Bach. His first big job came a year later when he was appointed organist to the Duke of Saxe-Weimar. He stayed in the job for nine years, although his relationship with his boss became more than a little rocky towards the end of his tenure when he asked to leave for another job after being passed over for promotion. The Duke became so fed up with him that Bach was thrown in jail for a month. It wasn't the first time that Bach had fallen out with his employers; he had upset the Church authorities in one of his previous roles. He was definitely one of those people who reacted very badly to being told what to do.

In the end, Bach got his way and left to join the court of Prince Leopold of Anhalt-Cöthen as "Kapellmeister" – the modern equivalent would be "Director of Music". Bach wrote much of his instrumental and orchestral music here. In 1720, his wife Maria died, but it didn't take Bach long to find a replacement, and his wedding to Anna Magdalena Wilcken took place just a year later.

In total, Bach had 20 children, although because of the high infant mortality rates at the time, only 9 survived beyond their early childhood. Of these, Wilhelm Friedemann, Carl Philippe Emanuel, Johann Christoph Friedrich and Johann Christian all became composers.

Bach moved on to a job at a school in Leipzig in 1723, where he spent the final 27 years of his life. It may come as a surprise now, but Bach was in fact the second choice for the job – with Telemann being offered it first. As well as teaching, Bach was organist and choirmaster in the local church. He was required to create a huge number of choral pieces, and it was hard work. Once again, Bach fell out with the authorities, although this time he opted to stick with the job until the bitter end.

Among the many wonderful pieces Bach wrote during this period of his life, the two Easter works – the *St John Passion* and the *St Matthew Passion* – particularly stand out. On a more light-hearted note, he also wrote *The Coffee Cantata* for a music group that met in a local coffee house.

Bach always had a strong interest in maths and liked to represent numbers in his music. He believed that 14 was his own personal number because that was the total his name scored when he added up the alphabetic position of each of its component letters. Patterns around the number 14 often appear in his music.

Towards the end of his life, Bach suffered from cataracts, and his eyesight began to fail. The English surgeon, John Taylor, botched an operation to cure the problem, just as he had done with Handel, and Bach was left almost totally blind. Just before Bach

died, something happened that corrected the problems in his eyes naturally, and for a short period he was able to see well enough to continue working on his final piece, *The Art of Fugue*.

Bach's rate of composition was quite remarkable, and after he died it took no less than 46 years to collect and publish all of his works.

At a glance: George Frideric Handel

Born:	1685
Died:	1759
Nationality:	Initially German and then English
Must listen:	*Messiah*; "*Ombra Mai Fù*" from the opera *Xerxes*; "*Zadok the Priest*" (used in the film *The Madness of King George*); *Water Music*; *Arrival of the Queen of Sheba* from the oratorio *Solomon*

You can hear an excerpt from "*Zadok the Priest*" on **CD Track 6**. See page 189 for more information.

Handel's father was not at all keen on his son taking up music as a career, and he banned the young boy from having anything to do with it, preferring him to study law before ending up with a sensible, secure job. Handel's mother, on the other hand, seemed to recognize talent when she heard it. History has it that she smuggled a small harpsichord into the attic of their home, where

George Frideric would practise away, out of his father's earshot.

When Handel was eight years old, the Duke of Saxe-Weissenfels heard him play. The Duke was so impressed that he ensured that the boy had lessons. Such was Handel's natural talent that just three years later his tutor said that there was nothing left that he could teach him. Remarkably, this appears to have been the last time that Handel had formal music tuition; he was eleven.

In his late teens, Handel took up a role as an organist before moving to Hamburg, where he tried his hand at writing opera. He decided to move to Italy in order to better learn that particular skill.

After around four years soaking up as much of the Italian music scene as he possibly could, Handel travelled to Hanover, where he was given a position in the court of the Elector.

The travel bug had well and truly bitten though, and Handel asked for permission to visit England. His request was granted and he set off across the English Channel. Handel was a big hit in London, and his opera *Rinaldo* was greeted with universal acclaim – even though he had written it in just 15 days. Although he did eventually return to Germany, Handel later travelled again to London, where he repeated his initial success.

By now, Handel was really pushing his luck as far as his employer was concerned. He was still on the payroll in Hanover, yet spent all his time away from the court. Suddenly, everything changed for him – and it was a change for the better.

The English monarch, Queen Anne, died. The heir to the throne was Handel's boss, the Elector of Hanover, who became King George I. The new king forgave Handel's absence, employing him in London. Handel must have felt at home in the city because this was the period when he wrote much of his greatest music, including in 1717 when he composed his *Water Music* for a royal pageant on the River Thames.

In 1727, George I died and Handel continued to compose for George II, with *"Zadok the Priest"* written as a coronation anthem. It has been sung at the coronation of every British monarch ever since.

Handel's *Music for the Royal Fireworks* was written for a display put on by King George II in London's Hyde Park. The music was a triumph, but the fireworks were an unmitigated disaster, with one particular Catherine wheel setting fire to a wooden tower and causing pandemonium among the crowds.

One of Handel's most performed works today is his oratorio, *Messiah*. By the way, an oratorio is usually a

religious story which has been set to music, a little like an opera, but normally without scenery and costumes. It is performed by solo singers, a choir and an orchestra.

Messiah was written in aid of three Irish charities and was given its premiere in Dublin in 1741. It includes the incredibly uplifting *Hallelujah Chorus*, which is heard regularly at Christmas and Easter today. It was another example of how speedily Handel could produce the goods when required; even though it lasts for two and a half hours, it took him just 24 days to write the music.

Handel was undoubtedly a complex character. He was grumpy, speaking English with a heavy accent and muttering constantly to himself in German; he had atrocious table manners and was a greedy eater; but that never stopped him from creating the most incredible music.

Handel's success is a fine example of classical music's ability to cross geographical divides. Here was a man who was born in Germany and yet became one of English music's greatest success stories, still being seen as part of the English establishment centuries after his death. If you ever visit Westminster Abbey, make sure you pause to pay tribute to Handel: his body still lies there today.

At a glance: Domenico Scarlatti

Born: 1685
Died: 1757
Nationality: Italian
Must listen: *Sonata in A Major K.182*

When you talk about Scarlatti, make sure you refer to the right one. We're focusing on **Domenico Scarlatti**, rather than his lesser-known father, Alessandro.

Scarlatti was by no means as great a composer as the previous two giants of the Baroque period, with whom he shared the same birth year. He was, however, a fine keyboard player, and much of his best work was for the keyboard. Scarlatti wrote 500 or so sonatas for the instrument.

Legend suggests that Scarlatti once had a keyboard duel with Handel. The former played the harpsichord and the latter, the organ. The judges appear to have sat on the fence when it came to naming a winner: Scarlatti was declared the better harpsichordist and Handel the better organist.

At a glance: Domenico Zipoli

Born: 1688
Died: 1726
Nationality: Italian
Must listen: *Elevazione*

Our final composer from the Baroque period is one of the least well documented, although he became far more famous in South America then he ever did in his native Italy. **Domenico Zipoli** was born in Naples but towards the end of his life he emigrated to Argentina. His *Elevazione* has become a big favourite of Classic FM listeners, and 200 years after his death new repertoire that Zipoli had written was still being discovered. In the 1970s, around 20 previously unknown works turned up in Bolivia; he must have composed them while serving as a Jesuit missionary in Paraguay.

The end of the Baroque period

Appropriately enough, Zipoli brings to an end our A to Z of composers from the Baroque period, which began back at the turn of the 17th century with Allegri. The Baroque composers marked 150 years of musical development. The influence of the Church at the end of the Baroque period was far less marked than it was at the end of the Early Music period. Kings, queens and noblemen were now major forces in commissioning new music and in employing musicians to perform it. This was the period when classical music became showbiz – even though showbiz wouldn't be invented for another couple of hundred of years.

There were, however, still a huge number of changes to come during the next period of classical music – a time that many people regard as being at the very heart of the whole genre.

04

The Classical Period

Isn't it all Classical?

Just in case you skipped the introduction to our *Friendly Guide*, this is a reminder that although everything we play on air on Classic FM is classical music, there was also a **Classical period** of classical music. It was neatly sandwiched between the Baroque period that we have just lived through, and the Romantic period, which is still to come. Broadly speaking, the Classical period runs from 1750 until 1830, so it is actually the shortest of all the periods that we cover in this book.

Don't for a moment think that because this particular period spanned only eight decades, it was in any way light on new developments, big names or stunning music. As you will see, it has all three by the bucket-load.

As well as embracing the three classical greats – Haydn, Mozart and Beethoven – the Classical period also saw the development of the classical symphony and concerto into the form that we would regard as being normal today. More and more, composers were also being thought of as stars in their own right, as classical music became a far wider pursuit among the middle classes.

What else was going on?

Scientific invention continued apace and the Industrial Revolution arrived in Britain. Steam was harnessed for the first time as a means of powering large-scale factory production. James Hargreaves came up with the "Spinning Jenny", which revolutionized the cotton industry, and Benjamin Franklin invented the lightning conductor.

Big strides were made in the world of transport: James Brindley designed the Worsley to Manchester Canal; the first railway opened from Stockton to Darlington; and man flew for the very first time when two French brothers, Joseph and Jacques

Montgolfier, created the first hot air balloon in 1783.

James Cook discovered Australia and, not long afterwards, the first convicts started being shipped out. Meanwhile, America gained its independence and France underwent a revolution, which resulted in it losing its monarchy.

Our classical top ten

In this chapter of our *Friendly Guide*, we will be concentrating on ten composers from the Classical period – some extremely well known, others less so. Yet all were influential on the development of the Classical period of classical music.

At a glance: Christoph Willibald von Gluck

Born:	1714
Died:	1787
Nationality:	German
Must listen:	*Orpheus and Euridice*

It is for his contribution to the opera world that **Christoph Willibald von Gluck** is best remembered today. Just as Purcell and Monteverdi had done before, Gluck took the story of *Orpheus and Euridice* and turned it into an opera. His style was very different from what had gone before, with a greater emphasis on characterization and story-telling. He also included two sections of ballet in the opera including *The Dance of the Blessed Spirits,* which remains very popular today.

Gluck cleaned opera up from being a vehicle for star singers to show off, to one that allowed the story to shine through. He was among the first composers to use clarinets, cor anglais (they look like over-sized oboes) and trombones in his operas.

Gluck died in Vienna after suffering a series of strokes. It is believed that his death was brought on by his insistence on drinking an after-dinner liqueur, even though his doctor had forbidden him to do so.

At a glance: Carl Philippe Emanuel Bach

Born: 1714
Died: 1788
Nationality: German
Must listen: *Harpsichord Concerto in D Minor,*
               "Magnificat"

Carl Philippe Emanuel Bach was born in the same year as Gluck. You would, of course, be right in thinking that the name sounds familiar. Carl Philippe Emanuel Bach was the son of Johann Sebastian Bach. Although he was nowhere near as important a composer as his father, Carl Philippe Emanuel did make a significant contribution to the

development of the classical sound, acting as a bridge between the Baroque style encapsulated by Johann Sebastian and the clearly different Classical style of composers such us Haydn and Mozart – of whom, more in a moment. Carl Philippe Emanuel's earliest works sounded very much like those of his father, whereas his later works were more similar to Haydn's.

During his lifetime, Carl Philippe Emanuel was famous as a keyboard player, working for King Frederick the Great for some 28 years. As a composer, he developed the sound of the sonata. He took over from Telemann as music director in Hamburg, where he was in charge of around 200 performances a year in 5 different churches. Carl Philippe Emanuel managed to find time to write a manual called *The Art of Keyboard Playing*, which was used by many of the pianists who followed him.

At a glance: Franz Joseph Haydn

Born:	1732
Died:	1809
Nationality:	Austrian
Must listen:	*The Creation* – a choral masterpiece; *Symphony No. 94 in G*; *Cello Concertos Nos. 1 & 2*; *The Seasons*

You can hear an excerpt from the "*Surprise*" *Symphony No. 94* on **CD Track 8**. See page 190 for more information.

Joseph Haydn was one of the great architects of the Classical period of classical music. He lived longer than many of his contemporaries and witnessed huge developments in the way that music was written during his 77-year life. Haydn was particularly influential in developing the symphony, sonata and string quartet, and was to become a major inspiration to those who followed him, including Mozart and Beethoven.

Haydn was another man with a tremendous creative urge, publishing around 1,200 works, including no fewer than 104 symphonies, more than 80 string quartets, over 50 piano sonatas, at least 24 concertos and 20 operas. Then there are nearly 90 choral works, more than 100 songs, plus literally hundreds of other pieces for solo instruments or chamber groups, all of which bore Haydn's name.

Back in Haydn's day, castrati were still a relatively common phenomenon. These were men, who, without putting too fine a point on it, had been operated upon to ensure that their voices never actually broke. Haydn had a magnificent singing voice as a boy and his choirmaster suggested that he could keep it forever if he would just undergo a very small operation. Haydn was happy to go along with the idea, until his horrified father found out what was about to happen and the boy was told what the operation would actually entail.

Haydn was able to compose so much principally because of the patronage of the Esterházy family, who were extremely influential within Hungarian society. He also became one of the first truly international musical figures, making tours around Europe, in the way that the Rolling Stones or Robbie Williams might do today. Haydn was particularly popular on his visits to England, and he had two long stays in the country at the end of his life. This allowed him to build up quite a treasure chest of riches – he was most certainly not the stereotypical impoverished composer whom we will meet so often later in our *Friendly Guide*.

Haydn's success is all the more remarkable because he appears, in the main, to have taught himself about music. This seems to have been a benefit, rather than a drawback, allowing him to develop his own style of composing, free from the constraints of the perceived wisdoms of the time.

It is for his symphonies that Haydn is most remembered today. Many of them were given nicknames, with fun stories attached as to how they got these names.

Take the *"Farewell" Symphony No. 45*, for example. This was composed while Haydn was working for the Esterházy family. The court musicians were fed up with being separated from their wives and families. Haydn wanted to get the message across to his boss, so the musical score instructed the musicians one by one to blow out the candles by their music stands and exit the stage. At the end, only the two principal violinists are left.

The nicknames go on, including *"The Clock"* *Symphony No. 101*, so called because of the tick-tocking slow movement, and the *"Surprise" Symphony No. 94*, with its deafening chord that comes crashing in after a very quiet opening. There are many others too: *"The Philosopher"*, *"Mercury"*, *"The Schoolmaster"*, *"The Bear"*, *"The Hen"*, *"The Miracle"*, and a whole group known as the *"London Symphonies"*.

At a glance: Johann Christian Bach

Born: 1735
Died: 1782
Nationality: German
Must listen: *Symphonies Op. 3,* which is actually made up of six works

During his lifetime, **Johann Christian Bach** was far more famous than his father, Johann Sebastian Bach, had been in his. Johann Christian's claim to fame was that he was the first person to give a solo piano performance in London, and he is sometimes referred to as "The London Bach".

Johann Christian made a lot of money early on his career, but things went wrong for him financially

towards the end of his life as his reputation started
to wane.

At a glance: Karl Ditters von Dittersdorf

Born: 1739
Died: 1799
Nationality: Austrian
Must listen: *Harp Concerto in A*

Karl Ditters von Dittersdorf does not appear in
our *Friendly Guide* because he was by any means the
most influential or creative composer of the
Classical period. In fact, many histories of classical
music don't include him at all. He is here as an act
of self-indulgence because of his wonderful name,
which has been a great favourite with Classic FM
presenters over the years.

Now largely forgotten, Dittersdorf was actually one
of the most popular composers in Europe during
his life, although he never managed to turn that
popularity into financial stability. He wrote more
than 120 symphonies and 45 operas, as well as
choral and chamber works. His music deserves to
have a wider hearing and, with a name like that, he
might just catch the public's imagination once
again.

He may have written around 600 different works,
but **Luigi Boccherini** is famous today for just one

At a glance: Luigi Boccherini

Born: 1743
Died: 1805
Nationality: Italian
Must listen: *String Quintet in E*; *Cello Concerto No. 9*

piece – the minuet from his *String Quintet in E*, which featured in the British cinema classic, *The Ladykillers*. Boccherini actually wrote 154 different quintets for various combinations of instruments.

During his lifetime, Boccherini was a star performer on the cello, touring Italy, France and Spain. His life ended unhappily though – he outlived his two wives and several of his children. He was himself unwell for some years, before eventually dying in poverty. Had he lived just a few years longer, Boccherini would have seen his music coming back in fashion.

At a glance: Antonio Salieri

Born: 1750
Died: 1825
Nationality: Italian
Must listen: *Flute and Oboe Concerto in C*

Our next composer is famous today for a crime he did not commit rather than for the music he wrote. However, for more than five decades, **Antonio**

Salieri was one of the most influential forces in the Viennese musical world. He enjoyed great success as an opera composer in Italy and France. Towards the end of his life, he concentrated on teaching.

Depending on your point of view, Salieri was either done a great disservice, or his place in history was secured by Pushkin's 1831 play *Mozart and Salieri* and Peter Schaffer's stunning 1984 film *Amadeus*.

To find out why, we need look no further than the very next composer in our *Friendly Guide*.

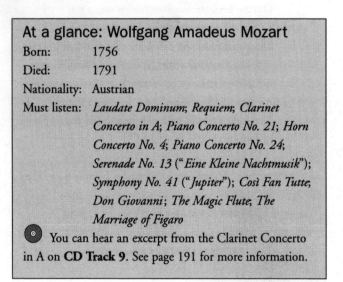

At a glance: Wolfgang Amadeus Mozart

Born: 1756
Died: 1791
Nationality: Austrian
Must listen: *Laudate Dominum*; *Requiem*; *Clarinet Concerto in A*; *Piano Concerto No. 21*; *Horn Concerto No. 4*; *Piano Concerto No. 24*; *Serenade No. 13* ("*Eine Kleine Nachtmusik*"); *Symphony No. 41* ("*Jupiter*"); *Così Fan Tutte*; *Don Giovanni*; *The Magic Flute*; *The Marriage of Figaro*

You can hear an excerpt from the Clarinet Concerto in A on **CD Track 9**. See page 191 for more information.

The argument rages between Mozart and Beethoven fans: which one was truly the greatest? At this moment in time, close to the 250th anniversary of

Mozart's birth, he appears to be in the ascendant. As we move towards the 200th anniversary of Beethoven's death in 2027, we may well see Beethoven rise to the top. There is little doubt in our minds at Classic FM, though, that along with Johann Sebastian Bach, Mozart and Beethoven are the true giants of classical music composition.

Johannes Chrysostomus Wolfgangus Amadeus Mozart was born in Salzburg on a snowy evening in January 1756. He was an incredible child prodigy, playing the piano at the age of three and composing by the time he was just four years old.

His father Leopold was a composer and musician who worked for the Prince Archbishop of Salzburg. His talent was nowhere near as great as that of his son, but music appears to have been in the Mozart family's blood, and Wolfgang's sister, Maria Anna (known as Nannerl), was a fine pianist.

When Leopold realized just how gifted his children were, he decided to take them on a tour of Europe. It was an epic journey that lasted for four years, taking in Munich, Vienna, Paris, London, Amsterdam, Munich again, and finally Salzburg.

Mozart was just six when the tour began and by its end he was a star, having played in front of the most influential people wherever he had been. Throughout his life, Mozart was a keen letter writer

and many of his notes to friends and family survive today, giving us an authentic glimpse into his life.

As a child, Mozart learned fast how to wow an audience and could do all sorts of tricks at the piano. One of his favourites was to play with his hands hidden under a cloth, so that he was unable to see any of the notes. But he didn't just excel at performing; by the time he was 12, he had already completed two operas.

It was time for Mozart to get back on the road again. On this occasion, the destination was Italy. The story goes that he heard a performance of Allegri's *Miserere* (see page 36). By papal decree, no printed parts existed for this work outside the confines of the Vatican. The young Mozart was so moved by the piece though that he rushed off and scribbled the whole work down onto manuscript paper, note perfect. This was a feat of pure musical genius.

While he was in Italy, Mozart was fascinated by the native opera composers and, by the end of his life, he himself had written some of the greatest examples of the genre, including *The Marriage of Figaro*, *Don Giovanni*, *Così fan tutte* and *The Magic Flute*.

Joseph Haydn was one of the great musical influences on Mozart's career, and each man was an unashamed fan of the other's work. Haydn told Mozart's father:

I must tell you before God and as an honest man, that your son is the greatest composer I ever heard of.

As a teenager, Mozart began working for the Prince Archbishop of Salzburg. It was always destined to be a troubled relationship, which culminated years later in Mozart literally being kicked out of the job with a boot up his backside.

Mozart had spent his early years being lauded as a genius, and this took its toll on his relationships with those around him. He could be incredibly arrogant, and went through his life exhibiting a talent for upsetting people and making enemies.

In love, Mozart was both pragmatic and persistent. When a young lady called Aloysia Weber spurned his advances, he turned his attention to her sister, Constanze, instead. A year later, they were married and had children of their own. They stayed together for the rest of Mozart's life in a very strong and loving marriage.

Some composers need to spend hours working and re-working every note that they write, but Mozart was a very speedy composer, creating intensely tuneful melodies from scratch, seemingly plucking them out of the air at every turn. Once, when he was walking along the street, a beggar asked him for some money. Instead of tossing him a coin, he wrote out a tune on a piece of manuscript paper,

telling the beggar to take it to a music publisher, who would exchange it for cash. Mozart himself said:

I write as a sow piddles.

Mozart was terrible when it came to looking after his finances. He worked hard and earned well for many years, but no matter how fast the money came in, he would always spend more than he had. During his final years, he was heavily in debt to many of his friends, who had no hope of ever seeing their loans again.

In the final year of his life, Mozart's health gradually dete¯iorated and there are all sorts of conspiracy theories about how Mozart came to die, including the idea that he was murdered by Antonio Salieri (as suggested in the play *Mozart and Salieri* and the film *Amadeus*). The story goes that a "masked stranger" came to Mozart's door and commissioned him to write a requiem. The shadowy figure at the door was not in fact Salieri, but was instead a servant of a nobleman, who probably intended to pass off Mozart's work as his own. Mozart began to believe that the "masked stranger" was the devil himself and that the requiem was in fact his own. As he worked on the piece, his health worsened and he never managed to finish it. The final parts were completed by his pupil, Süssmayr.

Mozart left his finances in a parlous state when he died at the tragically young age of 35. He was buried in an unmarked grave just outside Vienna, leaving behind more than 650 different works, which showed his mastery of every type of classical music. Opera, symphonies, concertos, chamber works, choral pieces: whatever he turned his hand to, Mozart could write with aplomb. It was a sad end to a truly great composer's life.

At a glance: Ludwig van Beethoven

Born:	1770
Died:	1827
Nationality:	German
Works:	398
Must listen:	*Symphony No. 5*, which must have the most famous opening bars in all classical music; *Symphony No. 6 ("Pastoral")*; *Symphony No. 9 ("Choral")*; *Moonlight Sonata*; *Für Elise*; *Violin Concerto*; *Piano Concerto No. 5 ("Emperor")*; *Fidelio*

You can hear an excerpt from *Symphony No. 5* on **CD Track 10**. See page 191 for more information.

It seems strange to have the two biggest names in classical music sit side by side in our *Friendly Guide*. It has not happened by design and is purely an accident of their dates of birth. However, in many people's view, the pinnacle of classical music appears in these few pages covering the lives of Mozart and

Beethoven. They may have a point, although there are plenty of gems still to come.

You may remember earlier on in our *Friendly Guide* how we discussed the rather inexact science of deciding exactly where a period of classical music begins and where it ends. Well, Beethoven's music is a case in point, with his life straddling the end of the Classical period and the beginning of the Romantic period that followed. To illustrate this, it's worth looking at his symphonies as an example. His *Symphony No. 1* very much follows the form of those Classical symphonies written by Haydn and Mozart, but by the time his *Symphony No. 9* was premiered, Beethoven was writing music that sounded very different indeed.

Ludwig van Beethoven liked to claim that the "van" in the middle of his name meant that he came from noble stock, but in fact he was descended from a perfectly normal family, with his ancestors originally coming from Holland.

There is no doubt that Beethoven had a tough childhood, though, and he was often beaten by his alcoholic father. He had obvious musical talent and his father was determined that he would become the "new Mozart".

Joseph Haydn taught Beethoven for a period, saying of him:

This young man will in time fill the position of one of Europe's greatest composers, and I shall be proud to be able to speak of myself as his teacher.

Unfortunately, Beethoven could be every bit as arrogant as Mozart – if not worse. He said Haydn was a teacher:

. . . from whom I learned absolutely nothing.

Beethoven was born 14 years after Mozart, and the young Ludwig played for Wolfgang, who was by then an adult. Mozart was impressed, saying:

Keep your eye on him; one day he will make the world talk of him.

In his twenties, Beethoven began to have trouble with his hearing, and by his forties he was completely deaf. He continued to create works of outstanding musicality and originality, without ever being able to hear a single note played. It is one of the most remarkable achievements in this whole book, and Beethoven should be marked as among the very greatest classical composers for that reason alone. Yet Beethoven does not need to be shown any favours because of his disability. The music that he created has stood the test of time and is regarded as among the greatest in the entire classical repertoire.

Although Beethoven refused to be defeated by his deafness, he did have trouble coming to terms with it. He would angrily thump the piano in an effort to hear the notes, sometimes even breaking the strings inside. He became an increasingly difficult person to be around, often drinking heavily, and he began to look increasingly unkempt, with wild hair and scruffy clothes.

Just as Mozart had done before him, Beethoven mastered a wide range of different types of classical music: from concertos to choral works; and from string quartets to pieces for solo instruments. He was a great concert pianist and wrote with an absolute understanding of what the instrument could achieve. Beethoven's best-known work for solo piano, the *Moonlight Sonata*, wasn't given the name by Beethoven himself, acquiring it instead from a critic, who thought that the piece evoked an image of the moon over Lake Lucerne.

Unlike Mozart, Beethoven tended to take a long time to write each of his pieces. Mozart was able to dash off a new work incredibly quickly, whereas Beethoven liked to spend ages working on a new tune. He would often work things out in his head, before finally writing it down. Then he would spend a long time crossing things out and trying new ideas, before eventually settling on what he wanted.

Beethoven composed only one opera – *Fidelio* – and it took him years to get it right. He re-wrote one aria no fewer than 18 times and came up with four different overtures before he settled on one that he liked.

Beethoven's speciality was the symphony – the style of which he developed hugely during his lifetime. For many, his final *Symphony No. 9* was his biggest triumph, with a much larger orchestra, a choir and four soloists. It includes the magnificent final movement, the *"Ode to Joy"*.

By the time this piece was first performed in public, Beethoven was completely deaf. On the big night, he stood on the stage with his back to the audience. At the end of the concert, it was only when one of the singers turned him around to face the crowd that he realized that they had been wildly cheering and applauding his masterpiece.

Beethoven was 56 years old when he died. His funeral was very different to that of Mozart. More than 30,000 people came out onto the streets to say goodbye. His torch-bearers included Franz Schubert, of whom more later.

Beethoven was a musical innovator. He led a troubled private life and never married, even though he fell hopelessly in love with a series of women. Coupled with his deafness, Beethoven often had an unhappy

time of it and he regularly became consumed with anger. Listening to music such as the *Moonlight Sonata*, this seems hard to believe. But, sadly it is true.

> ## At a glance: Louis Spohr
>
> | | |
> |---|---|
> | Born: | 1784 |
> | Died: | 1859 |
> | Nationality: | German |
> | Must listen: | *Clarinet Concerto No. 1 in C Minor* |

Our final composer from the Classical period is almost completely eclipsed by the likes of Mozart and Beethoven but nevertheless he was still an innovator in his own way. In fact, **Louis Spohr** was something of a revolutionary on the quiet. As well as being one of the first conductors to use a baton to keep time, he also invented the chin rest for the violin, some time around 1820.

Not only was he a well-respected composer, but Spohr was also a brilliant violinist in his day. Widely admired as a teacher, his book, *Violin Tutor*, became required reading. Spohr was another of those composers whose output had one foot in the Classical period and the other in the Romantic period.

The end of the Classical period

It may be the shortest period in our *Friendly Guide*, but this was a time that was by no means lacking in stature or importance in the overall development of classical music. The Classical years were marked out by some of the true greats. For the first time, composers became star names in their own right and, by the start of our next period, classical music had changed beyond all recognition from the style and forms that were the norms at the end of the Baroque period just 80 years before.

Gird your loins. It's time to get Romantic.

The Romantic Period

Why Romantic?

The **Romantic period** of classical music ran from around 1830 to 1910 or so. As with many labels used in this book, a strict definition of why Romantic music is romantic is quite hard to come by. There are parts of music written in all of the periods we cover in our *Friendly Guide* that could be considered to be "romantic".

The composers whose work falls into this category tend to bring emotions to the fore in their music, and often use the notes they write to paint pictures in a very expressive way. This is different to those composers who came before them in the Classical period. For them, writing music tended to be about having a formal structure, or framework, within which to compose.

Having said all of this, there are composers from the Classical period who have elements of Romanticism in their music, just as there are composers from the Romantic period who have elements of Classicism in their music. Really, there is no hard and fast rule, just a series of general indicators.

What else was going on in the world?

History didn't stand still just because everyone was going all Romantic. Inventions during this period included socialism, postage stamps and the Salvation Army. Vitamins and radium were discovered; the Suez Canal opened; Mr Daimler produced his first motor car; and the Wright brothers flew in their flying machine. Radio was born when Marconi successfully sent a message by wireless to a receiver over a mile away; Queen Victoria celebrated her jubilee; and the Great Gold Rush got underway.

The three ages of the Romantics

As you flick through our *Friendly Guide*, you might notice that this is the most substantial of all of the chapters so far, with no fewer than 37 composers included. Much of the music was composed in different countries simultaneously, and many of the composers' lives overlapped. To keep things as *friendly* as possible, we have divided this chapter into three sections: "The Early Romantics", "The Nationalists" and "The Late Romantics".

As you have probably come to expect by now, these sub-groupings are themselves not an exact science, but we feel that by dividing up the composers in this way, the story unfolds logically, although not always quite chronologically.

The Early Romantics

These are the composers who bridged the gap between the Classical period and the later Romantic period. Many of them were alive at the same time as the Classical composers, and they were certainly influenced by the likes of Mozart and Beethoven. However, all of them moved on the development of classical music in their own way.

Our first composer from the Romantic period was a superstar in his lifetime. During his performances, he was the consummate showman, able to perform

At a glance: Niccolò Paganini

Born: 1782
Died: 1840
Nationality: Italian
Must listen: *Violin Concerto No. 1 in D*; *Violin Concerto
             No. 2 in B Minor*

 You can hear an excerpt from the *Violin Concerto No.
1* on **CD Track 11**. See page 192 for more information.

all sorts of stunts using his violin. In the same way
that Jimmy Hendrix could amaze audiences more
than a century later as a rock guitar virtuoso,
Niccolò Paganini was able to stun those who saw
him perform with his outrageous playing.

Paganini could play complete works with just two
strings on his violin instead of four. Sometimes, he
would even deliberately snap some of the strings
mid-performance – and still play the piece
brilliantly.

Paganini's childhood was completely centred on
music, and his father would punish him for not
practising by withdrawing food and water.

As an adult, Paganini's playing was so good that
there were even stories suggesting that the only way
anybody could possibly play the violin that well was
if they had entered into a pact with the Devil.
When he died, the Church initially refused to allow

Paganini's body to be buried on their land for this reason.

Paganini himself was in no doubt about the benefits of being seen as a showman, saying:

I'm not handsome, but when women hear me play, they come crawling to my feet.

At a glance: Carl Maria von Weber

Born:	1786
Died:	1826
Nationality:	German
Must listen:	*Clarinet Concerto No. 1 in F Minor*

The style and structure of music was continuing to develop in the operatic world just as it was in music written for instrumentalists. In Germany, **Carl Maria von Weber** was at the vanguard of developments, although he lived outside the years that many people consider to be the Romantic period.

Opera was the family business as far as Weber was concerned, and he spent his childhood touring with the opera company that his father had set up. His opera *Der Freischütz* sealed his place in German musical history because of its use of folk tunes in the score. You will see a little later in our *Friendly Guide* that this is an idea that

became increasingly common in the Romantic period.

Weber also wrote a couple of cracking clarinet concertos – and it is for these that he is chiefly remembered today.

At a glance: Gioacchino Rossini

Born: 1792
Died: 1868
Nationality: Italian
Must listen: *The Barber of Seville*; *The Thieving Magpie*;
             William Tell; *Stabat Mater*

Italy is the home of opera and in **Gioacchino Rossini** the Italians had a new hero. He wrote both comic and tragic operas to equal acclaim.

Rossini was another of those composers who created new works very quickly, and it never seemed to take him longer than a few weeks to write an opera. At the height of his creative powers, he once said:

Give me a laundry list and I will set it to music.

Rossini claimed to have composed the whole of *The Barber of Seville* in just 13 days. His fast work rate meant that he had a stream of new operas premiering in opera houses across Italy. He did not

always get on well with the interpreters of his creations, though, saying:

How wonderful the opera world would be if there were no singers.

Then, at the age of 37, Rossini suddenly stopped writing opera altogether, and in the final three decades of his life his only major work was the choral piece *Stabat Mater*. It's never been quite clear why he decided to do this, although by then his bank balance was particularly healthy following on from his enormous critical and financial successes around Europe.

Aside from the music, Rossini was a great lover of food and his name has been appended to more dishes than any other composer. Omelette Rossini and Salade Rossini sit alongside the ubiquitous Tournedos Rossini on menus. In case you're wondering, the last dish is made from steak layered on croutons with foie gras and truffles on top.

Now, our next composer liked to party the night away as much as the next chap, but he was by no means a slacker when it came to doing his day job.

He may have only lived for 31 years, but **Franz Schubert** was a highly proficient composer by the time he was 17, and he still managed to leave behind more than 600 songs (known as "Lieder").

At a glance: Franz Schubert

Born: 1797
Died: 1828
Nationality: Austrian
Must listen: *Marche Militaire No. 1*; Overture and
               Incidental Music to *Rosamunde*; *Piano
               Quintet* (*"Trout"*); *Piano Sonata No. 21*;
               Symphony No. 8 (*"Unfinished"*)

Schubert also composed eight and a half symphonies, 11 operas and around 400 other pieces. In 1815 alone, he composed 144 songs, two masses, a symphony and a selection of other works.

All that composing didn't prevent Schubert from having a good time and he was famous for his musical parties, or "Schubertiads", as they were known.

Schubert contracted syphilis in 1823 and died of typhus just five years later in 1828. A year earlier, he had taken part in the funeral of his great hero Ludwig van Beethoven.

Interestingly, Schubert was one of the first major composers who relied on other people to promulgate their music. He himself only ever gave one major concert, in the year of his death, and this was overshadowed by Paganini, who had arrived in

Vienna at the same time. So poor old Schubert was never really given the credit he deserved in his lifetime or in the years that followed his death.

One of the great mysteries of Schubert's life is his *Symphony No. 8*, which is known as the *"Unfinished Symphony"*. He completed the first two movements, and then abandoned it. Nobody is quite sure why, but it still remains one of his most popular works today.

At a glance: Hector Berlioz

Born:	1803
Died:	1869
Nationality:	French
Must listen:	*Symphonie Fantastique*; *The Childhood of Christ*; *Requiem*

Hector Berlioz's father was a doctor, and Berlioz didn't receive the sort of hothoused musical education favoured by the parents of many of the other composers in our *Friendly Guide*.

Berlioz actually began to train in Paris as a doctor himself, but ended up spending more and more time sneaking off to the opera. In the end, he switched courses to study music, much to his family's disgust.

Berlioz was almost a caricature of how non-composers think a composer should be: very highly strung with

frequent temper tantrums; recklessly impulsive; capable of being intensely passionate; and, of course, absolutely hopelessly romantic when it came to falling in love. He once pursued an ex-lover with pistols and poison; he followed another disguised as a maid.

The principal object of Berlioz's desires was an actress called Harriet Smithson, whom he chased with a dedication that must have seriously unnerved her. He first saw her in a play in 1827, but didn't actually meet her until 1832. At first, she spurned his advances, and he wrote his *Symphonie Fantastique* as a response. They were finally married in 1833, but – true to form – he fell hopelessly in love with someone else within a few years.

When it came to writing music, Berlioz was not afraid to think big. Take his *Requiem,* for example. It was written for a huge orchestra and chorus, as well as four brass bands, one at each corner of the stage. This addiction to making everything as big as possible has not always stood Berlioz in good stead since his death. It means that it can be prohibitively expensive to stage his works in the way that he envisaged them because of the vast number of musicians who have to be paid. He knew his own mind, though, and composed with zeal, saying:

Every composer knows the anguish and despair occasioned by forgetting ideas which one has no time to write down.

At a glance: Felix Mendelssohn

Born: 1809
Died: 1847
Nationality: German
Must listen: *O for the Wings of a Dove*; *Songs without
             Words*; *Symphony No. 4 ("Italian")*; *Violin
             Concerto*; *Hebrides Overture*; *A Midsummer
             Night's Dream*

Anyone reading this book who has not yet left
school, would be forgiven for feeling a pang of
jealousy when they come across the likes of **Felix
Mendelssohn**. He was, as we have seen before in
these pages, and will see again before the end of our
story, a child prodigy.

Mendelssohn didn't just excel at music, though; he
was one of those infuriating individuals who seem
to be brilliant at just about anything they try:
painting, poetry, sport, languages – he mastered
them all.

Mendelssohn was lucky in that he was born into a
wealthy family, who were part of Berlin's "arty set".
During his childhood, Mendelssohn met many of
the city's most talented artists and musicians in his
own home.

Mendelssohn made his public debut at the age of
nine and by the time he was sixteen he had

composed his *Octet for Strings*. A year later, he wrote his overture to Shakespeare's *A Midsummer Night's Dream*. It was to be another 17 years before Mendelssohn would complete the rest of his incidental music for the same play (including the *Wedding March*, which is a feature of many marriage services today).

Mendelssohn was a cultured man with a happy, stable marriage and five children. He worked hard and travelled widely, including to Scotland. He didn't seem to think too much of the place, saying:

. . . [they] brew nothing but whisky, fog and foul weather.

This did not stop him from writing two of his most loved works about the country. His *Scottish Symphony* was composed 13 years after his first trip there, and his *Hebrides Overture* is based in some parts on Scottish folk tunes. Mendelssohn had other links to Britain, with his oratorio *Elijah* receiving its premiere in Birmingham in 1846. He even became friendly with Queen Victoria, and was Prince Albert's piano teacher for a short while.

Mendelssohn died at the tragically young age of 38. There was no question that he was pushing himself to the limit and was working too hard, but he never really got over the death of his beloved sister, Fanny, who was also a gifted musician.

At a glance: Frédéric Chopin

Born: 1810
Died: 1849
Nationality: Polish
Must listen: *Nocturne No. 2*; *Prelude No. 15* ("*The Raindrop*"); *Waltz No. 6* (*The "Minute" Waltz*); *Piano Concerto No. 1*

You can hear an excerpt from *The Raindrop Prelude* on **CD Track 12**. See page 193 for more information.

Here is another character who was a Romantic through and through. **Frédéric Chopin** did, however, show a dedication to one musical instrument, the like of which we see nowhere else in our *Friendly Guide*.

To say that Chopin loved the piano would be an understatement. He adored it, dedicating his life to taking piano composition and performance to new heights. In fact, he wrote virtually nothing else of note for any other instrument at all, other than when an orchestra was involved in a supporting role to a piano soloist.

Chopin was born in 1810 in Warsaw, to a French father and Polish mother. By the time he was just seven years old, he was already composing and performing; he never looked back.

Chopin became a fixture in Paris society, making very good money by teaching rich people how to play the piano. He was fastidious about how he looked and always careful to ensure that he was wearing the trendiest outfits.

As a composer, Chopin was particularly methodical. Not for him a hurried scribbling out of a new piece. Instead, composition was a rather painful and drawn-out process. He ended up writing 169 works for solo piano, and each one was finessed to perfection.

Chopin fell in love with the celebrated French writer with the remarkable name Amandine-Aurore-Lucile Dupin. She is better known under her male pseudonym, George Sand. She certainly sounds like a bit of a character, and could often be seen strutting about the streets of Paris wearing men's clothes and smoking a large cigar, much to the shock of the rest of polite society in the French capital. Chopin and Sand had a stormy relationship and eventually fell out of love.

Chopin was another of the Romantic composers who died young, claimed by tuberculosis at the age of 39, shortly after his relationship with Sand broke up.

Robert Schumann was yet another composer whose life was a tale of tragedy and early death, although in his case a dose of insanity was thrown in for good measure.

At a glance: Robert Schumann

Born:	1810
Died:	1856
Nationality:	German
Must listen:	*Scenes from Childhood No. 7 – Dreaming*; *Fantasie in C*; *Piano Concerto in A Minor*; the song cycle *Dichterliebe*

Schumann was a brilliant composer, but spent most of his life in the shadow of his wife **Clara Schumann**, who was one of the most famed pianists of the day. She was less well known as a composer, but wrote some very attractive music.

Schumann was unable to follow his dream of becoming a concert pianist because of an injury to his hand, and he was not always happy to live in the shadow of his wife's celebrity.

He is best remembered today for his piano pieces, his songs and his chamber music. Schumann suffered from syphilis and depression, trying to commit suicide by throwing himself into the River Rhine. He was placed in an asylum, where he died two years later.

Schumann was pragmatic about his art, saying:

In order to compose, all you have to do is remember a tune that nobody else thought of.

At a glance: Franz Liszt

Born: 1811
Died: 1886
Nationality: Hungarian
Must listen: *Hungarian Rhapsody No. 2; Liebestraum No. 3; Piano Sonata; Rhapsodie Espagnole*

If Paganini was the ultimate violin showman, then **Franz Liszt** steals the crown in the Romantic piano world. Liszt was also an influential teacher and was tireless in flagging up the work of other composers, particularly Wagner, whom we will meet later in our *Friendly Guide* (see page 118).

Liszt's piano compositions were fiendishly difficult to play – but he wrote them in the knowledge that he would be able to pull off even the seemingly impossible, because of his own brilliant musicianship.

As well as writing his own music, Liszt was adept at turning other people's big tunes into works for the piano. Pieces by Beethoven, Berlioz, Rossini and Schubert were all transcribed by Liszt, who then performed them with his customary style and panache. Considering that these pieces were originally written for an orchestra, it is remarkable how Liszt manages to make them sound totally complete, even though he had re-worked them for just one instrument.

Liszt was undoubtedly a superstar of his day and lived the rock 'n' roll lifestyle a good century or so before it was invented, with a string of sexual liaisons. His decision to take holy orders did nothing to dampen his ardour.

Liszt is also responsible for a change in concerts involving piano and orchestra, which is still in place today. He wanted his adoring fans to be able to see his hands flying up and down the keyboard, so he had the piano turned around. Before then, the pianists used to sit with their backs to the audience.

At a glance: Georges Bizet

Born: 1838
Died: 1875
Nationality: French
Must listen: *Carmen*; *The Pearl Fishers*; *L'Arlésienne Suite No. 1*; *Jeux d'Enfants*

You can hear an excerpt from *The Pearl Fishers Duet* on **CD Track 13**. See page 193 for more information.

He may be most famous for his opera *Carmen*, but as you will see from our list on page 199, Classic FM listeners are in no doubt as to **Georges Bizet**'s best work. *"Au Fond du Temple Saint"* (known as *"The Pearl Fishers Duet"*) from his opera *The Pearl Fishers* has consistently been the most popular operatic work in the Classic FM Hall of Fame, since we began the chart back in 1996.

Bizet was another of those children who excelled in all things musical at a very young age. He wrote his first symphony by the time he was just 17. He was also another composer who died tragically young, at the age of 36, probably of throat cancer.

Despite his great talent, poor old Bizet never really saw the success that he deserved in his own lifetime. *The Pearl Fishers* had a rocky start, and *Carmen* caused something of a moral outrage among Paris's chattering classes. It only really found favour with critics and audiences in the years after Bizet's death. Since then, it has been performed in the most important opera houses the world over.

The Nationalists

Here is another one of those inexact definitions for you. All of our Romantic composers, and indeed many of our Baroque and Classical composers, could be argued to be "nationalist" in one way or another.

However, we have grouped together the next 14 major composers (all from the Romantic period) because their music is written in a certain style that enables listeners who know a little about their classical music to identify the country of origin.

Sometimes these individual groups are referred to as "nationalist schools of composers". This is not a bad description – but think dolphins, rather than

children sitting in a classroom. A school of dolphins appears to swim together in the same overall direction, although once you look very closely, you see that each of the animals takes a slightly different route, jumping up, diving down, or moving from left to right at different times to their fellow dolphins. It works exactly the same way with schools of composers – although they have common links, each is writing his own style of music.

The Russian school

At a glance: Mikhail Glinka

Born: 1804
Died: 1857
Nationality: Russian
Must listen: *Ruslan and Ludmilla*; *Kamarinskaya*

If Russian music has a father figure, then **Mikhail Glinka** is the man. Nationalist composers incorporated the folk music of their native lands into their own music, and Glinka was influenced by the folk tunes that he was introduced to by his grandmother.

Unlike so many of the prodigies who litter these pages, Glinka only took up music in a serious way in his late teens and early twenties. His first proper job was a civil servant in the Ministry of Communications.

When he decided on a change of career, Glinka visited Italy, where he worked as a pianist. It was while he was there that he developed a deep love of opera. When he returned home, he penned his own first opera, *A Life for the Tsar*. Glinka was instantly heralded as the finest Russian composer of the time. His second opera, *Ruslan and Ludmilla*, was nowhere near as successful immediately, although it has stood the test of time better.

At a glance: Alexander Borodin

Born: 1833
Died: 1887
Nationality: Russian
Must listen: *Polovtsian Dances* from *Prince Igor*; *In the Steppes of Central Asia*; *String Quartet No. 2*

Alexander Borodin was another composer who had a working life outside of music. In fact, he was a much respected scientist. His first published work went under the splendid title: *On the Action of Ethyl-iodide on Hydrobenzamide and Amarien*. You will never hear it played on Classic FM, though, because it was a scientific paper and nothing to do with music at all.

Borodin was actually the illegitimate son of a Georgian prince. His mother cultivated Borodin's love of music and the arts in general, a passion that he managed to continue to develop throughout his life. He only had around 20 or so works published because he was so busy doing his day job, but these included symphonies, songs and chamber music.

Along with **Mily Balakirev, Nikolai Rimsky-Korsakov, César Cui** and **Modest Mussorgsky**, Borodin made up a group of Russians known as "The Mighty Handful". Their success was all the more remarkable because all of them actually had jobs away from the world of music – a big difference between them and virtually all of the other composers in our *Friendly Guide*.

Borodin is best known now for the *Polovtsian Dances* from his only opera, *Prince Igor*. It's worth pointing out that he never completed the opera himself (even though he spent 17 years working on it), and his friend Rimsky-Korsakov actually finished it off. More about him on page 102.

At a glance: Modest Mussorgsky

Born:	1839
Died:	1881
Nationality:	Russian
Must listen:	*Night on the Bare Mountain*; *Pictures at an Exhibition*; *Boris Godunov*

For our money, Modest Mussorgsky was the most inventive and influential of "The Mighty Handful", although he shared one or two of the demons that seem to be very common among truly creative people.

After leaving the army, Mussorgsky became a civil servant. In his younger days, he was quite a man about town, but he had a fiery temper and struggled with alcoholism throughout his adult life. For this reason, he is often pictured looking dishevelled with an unnaturally bright red nose.

Mussorgsky would often start writing pieces that were never finished. Sometimes, friends would try to help him out by completing them for him, although we can never be quite sure that these pieces actually turned out in the way he initially planned them. Rimsky-Korsakov orchestrated much of Mussorgsky's opera, *Boris Godunov*, and his big hit, *Night on a Bare Mountain* (which featured in the Disney film *Fantasia*). Mussorgsky's *Pictures at an Exhibition* was orchestrated by Maurice Ravel some years after Mussorgsky originally penned it – and it is this version that has stood the test of time.

Despite coming from a wealthy background and having huge talent both as a composer and as a pianist, Mussorgsky died in drink-induced poverty at the age of just 42.

At a glance: Nikolai Rimsky-Korsakov

Born: 1844
Died: 1908
Nationality: Russian
Must listen: *Scheherezade*; *Flight of the Bumble Bee*;
             Capriccio Espagnol

Nikolai Rimsky-Korsakov's family expected him to go into the navy, and he did not disappoint. They were a little more surprised when he gave up his life on the ocean wave to become a composer and music professor a few years later. In fact, Rimsky-Korsakov had been writing music all along and even started composing his *Symphony No. 1* while at sea, stationed for part of the time off Gravesend in the Thames Estuary. This has to be one of the least glamorous composing locations for any piece of music anywhere in this book.

As well as being remembered for his work in sorting out Mussorgsky's music, Rimsky-Korsakov wrote 15 operas of his own, all of which centred around Russian themes, although he was also influenced by music from further afield. We can particularly hear this in his greatest work, *Scheherezade*, which is based on the story of *The Arabian Nights*. Rimsky-Korsakov had a real skill for writing music that showed off orchestras at their very best. In his work as a music professor, he wrote extensively on this subject, and

influenced many of the Russian composers who
followed him – most notably Stravinsky.

At a glance: Pyotr Ilyich Tchaikovsky

Born: 1840
Died: 1893
Nationality: Russian
Must listen: *The Nutcracker*; *1812 Overture*; *Piano
            Concerto No. 1*; *Symphony No. 6
            ("Pathétique")*; *Romeo and Juliet*; *Sleeping
            Beauty*; *Swan Lake*; *Violin Concerto*

You can hear an excerpt from Tchaikovsky's greatest
triumph, *The 1812 Overture*, on **CD Track 14**. See page
194 for more information.

Pyotr Ilyich Tchaikovsky took the Russian folk
tunes favoured by the Russian nationalist composers,
but he did something else with them, infusing them
with other influences from across Europe.

Tchaikovsky led a tortured life, principally because
of his homosexuality, and he died in mysterious
circumstances. He himself said:

*Truly there would be reason to go mad if it were not
for music.*

He was a delicate child and throughout adulthood
was prone to depression, exhibiting suicidal
tendencies on more than one occasion. After

studying law, Tchaikovsky was employed briefly as a civil servant before leaving to further his musical studies. He made the mistake of getting married when he was 37 – a relationship that seems to have taken a terrible toll on both him and his wife. She ended up going mad and spending her last years in an asylum. For his part, Tchaikovsky became further depressed following the break-up of the relationship just two months after the wedding.

Tchaikovsky was particularly wounded by the poor reception given to his early compositions, and bad reviews also affected his mental state. It is ironic that many of the works involved, such as his *Violin Concerto* and *Piano Concerto No. 1*, are great favourites today. Indeed, a recording of the *Piano Concerto No. 1* was one of the first classical records to achieve "gold disc" status, selling millions of copies.

Tchaikovsky wrote ten operas, including *Eugene Onegin*, and ballet scores such as *The Nutcracker*, *Sleeping Beauty* and *Swan Lake*. Listening to these, nobody can be in any doubt that Tchaikovsky had a massive talent for creating highly melodic, catchy tunes – which is one of the main reasons that his ballets are performed so often today. These great tunes are equally in evidence when you listen to Tchaikovsky's symphonies and piano concertos.

For many years, Tchaikovsky benefited from the generosity of a rich widow called Nadezhda von Meck, who funded his work on the condition that the two of them should never meet. If ever their paths did cross, they agreed that they would not even acknowledge one another.

It's not entirely clear how Tchaikovsky died. Officially, he was poisoned by drinking water infected by cholera, although there is a school of thought that thinks he deliberately took his own life because of fears over being embroiled in a homosexual scandal.

The Czech school

At a glance: Bedřich Smetana

Born: 1824
Died: 1884
Nationality: Czech
Must listen: *Vltava from Má Vlast*; *The Bartered Bride*

If Glinka is the father of Russian music, then **Bedřich Smetana** occupies the same role for Czech music.

He constantly wove Czech stories and places into his music. There is no better example of this than his most popular work *Má Vlast*, which translates as

"My Homeland". It is a homage to the country of his birth, which took Smetana eight years to complete. Today, the most popular of the work's six sections is *Vltava*, which tells the story of the passage of the River Vltava through Prague.

Smetana ended up suffering from syphilis, deafness and, ultimately, insanity. He was, however, a huge influence on our next composer, **Antonín Dvořák**, although the latter's music won acclaim far outside Czech borders.

At a glance: Antonín Dvořák

Born:	1841
Died:	1904
Nationality:	Czech
Must listen:	*Symphony No. 9 ("New World"); Rusalka; Serenade for Strings; Slavonic Dances; Cello Concerto*

Dvořák was a Czech hero, and he loved his homeland and its people with the same passion with which they adored him.

Dvořák's music was championed by the great Johannes Brahms, who is one of the big players later in our *Friendly Guide* (see page 121). Gradually, Dvořák's fame spread around the world – he had a particularly solid fan base in England, with commissions coming from the Royal

Philharmonic Society and the Birmingham and Leeds Festivals.

Dvořák then decided to travel to the USA, where he was appointed Director of the National Conservatory of Music in New York in the 1890s. He was terribly homesick for the three years he was in the USA, but he did discover American folk music. He was influenced by these tunes when he was writing his *Symphony No. 9*, which carries the epithet *"From the New World"*. For an entire generation of British television viewers, the slow movement of this magnificent work will forever be known as "the Hovis music", after its use in a highly memorable television commercial for the bakery.

Dvořák felt the pull of his homeland throughout his time in the USA, and eventually he decided to go back home. He spent his final years working in Prague as a teacher.

Dvořák had one or two other interests outside music: he was an obsessive trainspotter and also developed a strong interest in ships. Indeed, this particular passion might have been one of the reasons he eventually agreed to travel to the USA in the first place, although the enormous riches on offer would have been another strong persuader.

- Other composers in the Czech nationalist school include: **Josef Suk, Leos Janácek** and **Bohuslav Martinů.**

107

The Scandinavian school

At a glance: Edvard Grieg

Born: 1843
Died: 1907
Nationality: Norwegian
Must listen: *Piano Concerto*; *Holberg Suite*; *Peer Gynt Suite No. 1* (includes *Morning* and *In the Hall of the Mountain King*)

The Norwegian **Edvard Grieg** was another of those composers who had a passionate love affair with their country of birth. And his fellow Norwegians loved him just as much as he loved them. It could so easily have been very different, though. Grieg was actually of Scottish descent – his great-grandfather emigrated to Scandinavia after the Battle of Culloden.

Grieg was best suited to writing small-scale works, such as his *Lyric Pieces* for solo piano, but his most famous concert work today is his beautiful *Piano Concerto*, which includes a very dramatic opening with notes pouring from the piano over the top of a drum roll.

- Other composers in the Scandinavian nationalist school include: **Carl Nielsen** and **Johan Svendsen**.

The Spanish school

At a glance: Isaac Albéniz

Born: 1860
Died: 1909
Nationality: Spanish
Must listen: *Suite Española No. 1*; *Iberia*

Although in the 19th century classical music was being written in Spain, the country was by no means a hotbed of famous composers. One exception is **Isaac Albéniz**, who was a bit of a tearaway as a youngster.

It's said that Albéniz could play the piano at just one year old. Three years later, he was performing in public, and by the age of eight, he was on the road plying his musical trade.

Albéniz was truly brilliant at improvising and could make up and vary tunes on the piano without a moment's thought. He often performed party pieces on the piano for money. He would stand with the keyboard behind him, and would play tunes with the backs of his hands. It is an incredibly difficult stunt to pull off. And, just for good measure, Albéniz used to do it dressed up as a musketeer, of all things. He had plenty of adventures as a youngster, and by the time he was 15 he had already performed in

countries as far apart as Argentina, Cuba, the USA and England.

As an adult, Albéniz led a far more conventional existence and became particularly famed for his very Spanish sounding solo piano work, *Iberia*. His success brought Spanish music out of the shadows and to the attention of international audiences.

- Albéniz was a big influence on many other composers from the Spanish nationalist school, including: **Pablo Martín de Sarasate, Enrique Granados, Manuel de Falla** and **Heitor Villa-Lobos** (who was actually Brazilian).

The English school

At a glance: Arthur Sullivan	
Born:	1842
Died:	1900
Nationality:	British
Must listen:	*HMS Pinafore*; *The Mikado*; *Ivanhoe*; *Symphony in E*

It's been a while since we have been in England. In fact, **Arthur Sullivan** is the first English composer we have featured in the Romantic period. Come to that, there were no English names whatsoever in the list that we covered in the Classical period. We have to wind the clock back to George Frideric Handel for our last English composer of note; he died in

1759, and we borrowed him from the Germans, if we are being strictly accurate on the subject of provenance. If you turn back through the pages, you will discover that it was Henry Purcell who was the last English-born composer in our *Friendly Guide* – and he began *de*-composing in 1695. We have had to wait an awfully long time before English composers have made it back onto the international stage.

The Germans were not slow in noticing England's failure to deliver the goods for a couple of hundred years. They took to referring to England as: "*The land without music*".

Arthur Sullivan is still famous today. However, history has been rather unfair to him because he is best known for what might not actually have been his best work. In the 1870s, Sullivan began a partnership with the librettist W.S. Gilbert. They collaborated on a series of light-hearted operettas, including: *Trial by Jury, The Pirates of Penzance, HMS Pinafore, Princess Ida, The Mikado* and *The Yeoman of the Guard.*

Despite their enormous success, the two men never really saw eye to eye and had a series of extremely heated rows. One of their most spectacular bust-ups was about a new carpet at the Savoy Theatre in London, where their operettas were usually staged.

Sullivan was desperate to be treated as a serious composer, but by and large his non-operetta works are now forgotten. He wrote an opera, *Ivanhoe*, and an attractive *Symphony in E*. He also wrote the tune to the hymn *"Onward! Christian Soldiers"*, which probably now counts as his most-performed work.

- Other composers in the English nationalist school include: **Arnold Bax, Hubert Parry, Samuel Coleridge-Taylor, Charles Villiers Stanford** and **George Butterworth**.

The French school

At a glance: Jacques Offenbach

Born:	1819
Died:	1880
Nationality:	French
Must listen:	*The Tales of Hoffman*; *Orpheus in the Underworld*

France's answer to Gilbert and Sullivan's English operettas came in the form of works by **Jacques Offenbach**, a man who obviously had a sense of humour. He was born in the town of Cologne and would sometimes sign himself as "O. de Cologne".

Offenbach also unleashed the *Can-Can* on an unsuspecting French public in 1858. The *Can-Can* comes from the operetta *Orpheus in the Underworld*, which scandalized the chattering classes of Paris at

the time of its premiere. If you think the title of this
work sounds familiar, then you would be right. It is
the same story that Peri, Monteverdi, Purcell and
Gluck all set to music in previous centuries.
Offenbach's version was very satirical, much more
fun than the previous incarnations, and was
riotously debauched in places. Despite the initial
shock, it proved to be very successful and
Offenbach never really looked back.

The other work for which he is most remembered is
the more serious opera, *The Tales of Hoffman*, which
features the *Barcarolle*.

At a glance: Léo Delibes

Born: 1836
Died: 1891
Nationality: French
Must listen: *Lakmé*; *Coppélia*; *Sylvia*

By no means as influential as Offenbach, **Léo
Delibes** is chiefly remembered now for his opera
Lakmé, which includes *The Flower Duet*. This was
used to great effect in a long-running British
Airways advertising campaign. Delibes also wrote
two notable ballets, *Coppélia* and *Sylvia*.

Delibes was not without influential friends – he
worked for both Berlioz and Bizet when he was
chorus master at Paris's Théâtre Lyrique.

- Other composers in the French nationalist school include: **Emmanuel Chabrier, Charles-Marie Widor, Joseph Canteloube** and **Jules Massenet**, whose opera, *Thaïs*, includes the *Meditation*, which has become a party piece for many violin soloists.

The Viennese waltz school

At a glance: Johann Strauss Sr

Born:	1804
Died:	1849
Nationality:	Austrian
Must listen:	*Radetzky March*

Our final two composers from among the Nationalist Romantics may well be father and son, but the time lag between the two generations was not great, with just 21 years separating the two men's birthdays. **Johann Strauss Sr** is known as "the father of the waltz". He was a fine violinist and set up an orchestra that toured all over Europe, with great financial success.

Johann Strauss Sr may have been "the father of the waltz", but it was Johann Strauss Jr who was to earn the title "the Waltz King". His father didn't want him to take up the violin, but Strauss Jr did so anyway, going on to set up a new orchestra to rival that of his father. Strauss Jr had a keen business brain and soon he was earning serious riches.

At a glance: Johann Strauss Jr

Born: 1825
Died: 1899
Nationality: Austrian
Must listen: *By The Beautiful Blue Danube*; *Die Fledermaus*;
             Tales from the Vienna Woods; *Tritsch-Tratsch
             Polka*; *Thunder and Lightning Polka*

You can hear an excerpt from *By the Beautiful Blue
Danube* on **CD Track 15**. See page 195 for more
information.

In the process, Strauss Jr wrote nearly 400 waltzes,
including the most popular of them all, *By The
Beautiful Blue Danube*. In the end, he had six
Strauss orchestras running simultaneously, two of
which were conducted by his brothers **Josef** and
Eduard (each of whom had around 300
compositions to his name).

Strauss Jr's waltzes and polkas were an instant hit in
the coffee houses of Vienna, and their light,
jaunty style proved to be popular all over Europe.
Classical music enthusiasts who take themselves
too seriously sometimes consider the Strauss
family's oeuvre to be beneath them. Don't let
them influence you! This family knew how to
write a great tune that can lift your spirits and
reverberate around your head for days after you first
hear it.

The Late Romantics

Many of our final group of Romantic composers were still composing music well into the 20th century, but they appear in this chapter rather than the next because they still have that Romantic sound to their work.

It is worth noting that many of these Romantic composers had strong friendships with some of the other composers discussed in "The Early Romantics" and "The Nationalists" sections of this chapter.

It also bears saying once again that there was so much great music being composed at the same time in different countries around Europe that any attempt to group the composers together in this way will be, to a certain extent, completely subjective. Although most reference books are very clear on which composers belong in the Baroque and Classical eras, things start to become a little fuzzier around the edges when it comes to the end of the Romantic period and the beginning of the 20th century.

In 19th-century Italy, one opera composer stood head and shoulders above all others: **Giuseppe Verdi**. With his big bushy moustache and beard, photographs show him with a glint in his eye.

At a glance: Giuseppe Verdi

Born: 1813

Died: 1901

Nationality: Italian

Must listen: *"Celeste Aida"* and *"The Grand March"* from *Aida*; Overture to *La Forza del Destino*; *"Questa o Quella"* and *"La Donna è Mobile"* from *Rigoletto*; *"Sempre Libera"* from *La Traviata*; *"Anvil Chorus"* from *Il Trovatore*; *"Chorus of the Hebrew Slaves"* from *Nabucco*; *"Dies Irae"* from the *Requiem*

You can hear an excerpt from the *"Anvil Chorus"* on **CD Track 17**. See page 196 for more information.

Verdi's operas are packed full of great tunes. In total, he wrote 26, most of which are still being performed today. They include many of the best-known operatic arias of all time.

Verdi was a big hit with opera audiences across Italy, and when *Aida* received its premiere, the standing ovation at the end was so prolonged that the company made no fewer than 32 curtain calls.

Nonetheless, there was sadness in Verdi's life, too. He outlived both of his wives and two of his children. His music generated considerable wealth and when he died he left his riches to a retirement home for musicians, which he had built in Milan.

He said that he regarded this as a greater work than all of his music.

Although he is best known for his operas, no discussion of Verdi's life would be complete without mention of his *Requiem*. It is regarded as one of the greatest pieces of choral music of all time. Although it was always intended to be a purely choral work, it is full of drama and rather operatic in style.

At a glance: Richard Wagner

Born: 1813
Died: 1883
Nationality: German
Must listen: Overture to *The Flying Dutchman*; Prelude
                to Act 3 of *Lohengrin*; *"Bridal Chorus"* from
                Lohengrin (which still features in many
                wedding ceremonies today); *"Ride of the
                Valkyries"* from *Die Walküre*; *"Siegfried's
                Funeral March"* from *Götterdämmerung*;
                "Pilgrims' Chorus" from *Tannhäuser*; Prelude
                to *Tristan and Isolde*

You can hear an excerpt from the *"Ride of the Valkyries"*
on **CD Track 18**. See page 196 for more information.

Our next composer was not a nice man. In fact, he was the most odious character with the most hateful views in the whole of our *Friendly Guide*. If we were choosing composers to include in this book in terms of their personalities, then **Richard Wagner**

simply would not make it. However, we are judging the music – not the man – and so no history of classical music is complete without his inclusion.

Wagner's brilliance as a composer is not in doubt. Some of the most important and impressive music of the whole of the Romantic period came from his pen, especially in the world of opera. Yet he was an anti-Semitic racist, a serial philanderer, who was prepared to lie, cheat and steal to get what he wanted, and he would ride rough-shod over people, casting them aside without further thought. Wagner had a monstrous ego, a vile temper, was wildly eccentric and appeared almost to believe that he was some form of deity.

It is for his operas that Wagner is chiefly remembered. He took German opera to a whole new level and, although he was born in the same year as Verdi, the sound he created was very different to that of the Italian operas of the same period.

One of Wagner's big ideas was to give each of his main characters a musical theme that recurred in the music at the points when they were at the forefront of the action. This seems very logical to anyone who is a fan of musicals today, but at the time it was a revolutionary idea.

Wagner's greatest triumph was *The Ring Cycle*, which is made up of four operas: *Das Rheingold*,

Die Walküre, Siegfried and *Götterdämmerung.*
These tend to be performed over four consecutive
nights and last well in excess of 15 hours. These
four operas represent a huge achievement for one
man and, just because we find his views so
objectionable, that should not take away from their
magnificence.

Length is something of a trademark for
Wagner's operas. His final opera, *Parsifal,* is well
over four hours long. The conductor, David
Randolph, said of it:

*The kind of opera that starts at six o'clock and after it
has been going three hours you look at your watch and
it says 6:20.*

At a glance: Anton Bruckner

Born:	1824
Died:	1896
Nationality:	Austrian
Must listen:	*Symphony No. 7*; *Symphony No. 8*

Anton Bruckner's life as a composer is a lesson in
never giving up. He was a hard worker, thinking
nothing of practising 12 hours a day in his job as an
organist. He taught himself much of what he knew
about music and only graduated from a
correspondence course on composition at the ripe
old age of 37.

Bruckner is most respected today for his symphonies – he wrote nine of them in total. He was sometimes racked with self-doubt, but he did at least achieve acclamation, although much later in life than he deserved. The critics finally told him they loved him following the premiere of his *Symphony No. 7*. He was 60 years old.

At a glance: Johannes Brahms

Born:	1833
Died:	1897
Nationality:	German
Must listen:	*Academic Festival Overture*; *Hungarian Dance No. 5*; *Piano Concerto No. 1*; *Symphony No. 4*; *Violin Concerto*

Johannes Brahms was not one of those composers born with a silver baton in their hands. Instead, he came from a relatively poor background, or at least from a good family who were no longer as rich as they had been. As a teenager, Brahms would earn money by playing the piano in brothels around his native Hamburg. It's fair to say that he had already seen something of the seedier side of life by the time he was an adult.

Brahms's music was championed by Robert Schumann, and the two men became friends. When Schumann died, Brahms grew closer to Clara Schumann, eventually falling passionately in love

with her. It's not clear exactly how close they became, although Brahms's relationship with her may have coloured his judgement of other women, because nobody else seems to have held the same significance in his affections.

Brahms was quite a curt and short-tempered man, but his friends claimed that he had a softer side, which he did not always show towards strangers. On his way out of a party, he once said:

If there is anyone here whom I have not insulted, I beg his pardon.

Brahms would not have won any prizes in a "best turned-out composer" competition. He hated to buy new clothes and often wore baggy trousers that were covered in patches and nearly always too short. On one occasion, his trousers nearly fell down altogether in the middle of a performance. Another time, he was forced to take off his tie and use it as a belt to keep his trousers from ending up around his ankles.

Brahms's musical style owes much to the influences of Haydn, Mozart and Beethoven, and some music experts believe him to be a composer who still wrote in the style of the Classical period some years later than was strictly fashionable. Having said that, Brahms did introduce some new ideas. He was particularly adept at developing small groups of

notes in his music and stretching them out throughout the piece – what musicians call a "recurring motif".

Brahms was not an opera man, but otherwise wrote excellent examples of just about every other genre of classical music. This has, quite rightly, meant that he is regarded as one of the giants among the composers in the whole of this chapter. His own view on his work was to the point:

It is not hard to compose, but it is wonderfully hard to let the superfluous notes fall under the table.

At a glance: Max Bruch

Born: 1838
Died: 1920
Nationality: German
Must listen: *Violin Concerto No.1*; *Scottish Fantasy*; *Kol Nidrei*; *Symphony No. 3*

You can hear an excerpt from the *Violin Concerto No. 1 in G Minor* on **CD Track 16**. See page 195 for more information.

Born just five years later than Brahms, **Max Bruch** would have been completely eclipsed by his fellow German had it not been for one piece of music – his *Violin Concerto No.1 in G Minor*.

Bruch himself recognized this fact when he said, with a modesty that is rare among composers:

50 years from now, Brahms will loom up as one of the supremely great composers of all time, while I will be remembered for having written my G Minor Violin Concerto.

How right he was. But, what a piece to be remembered for! Bruch did compose many other works – around 200 in all – especially a number of big choral pieces and some operas, which tend not to be performed that often today. His music is big on tunes, but he did nothing to really break new ground. In fact, he was not that keen on the music of his fellow composers who were trying to innovate.

In 1880, Bruch was appointed conductor of the Royal Liverpool Philharmonic Orchestra, but three years later he was back in Berlin. The orchestra's players were not great fans.

At a glance: Camille Saint-Saëns

Born:	1835
Died:	1921
Nationality:	French
Must listen:	*The Carnival of the Animals*; *Danse Macabre*; *Violin Sonata No. 1 in D Minor*; *"Organ" Symphony No. 3*

We have already come across a galaxy of prodigious stars, but **Camille Saint-Saëns** arguably tops the lot. When he was just two years old, Saint-Saëns could already play tunes on the piano – and he had mastered reading and writing, too. A year later, he started to pick out his own compositions on the piano. Just four years after that, he had added a mastery of lepidoptery to his talents (that's the study of insects). By the time he was ten, Saint-Saëns had no problem at all in playing piano works by Mozart and Beethoven. His other areas of expertise included geology, astronomy and philosophy. There was no getting away from it – he was a clever kid.

After studying at the Paris Conservatoire, Saint-Saëns worked as an organist for many years. As he got older, he became more influential in French musical life, and ensured that the music of composers such as J.S. Bach, Mozart, Handel and Gluck all received regular performances.

Saint-Saëns's best-known work is *The Carnival of the Animals*, which he banned from public performance during his lifetime. He was worried that he would not be taken seriously as a composer once the critics heard it. It's great fun, with the orchestra depicting a lion, hens and cocks, tortoises, an elephant, kangaroos, an aquarium, birds, donkeys, pianists, fossils and a swan.

Some of Saint-Saëns's other music was written for less often heard combinations of instruments, including his famous *"Organ" Symphony No. 3*, which was used in the film *Babe*.

At a glance: Gabriel Fauré

Born: 1845
Died: 1924
Nationality: French
Must listen: *Requiem*; *Cantique de Jean Racine*; *Dolly Suite*; *Claire de Lune*; Incidental music to *Pelléas et Mélisande*

Saint-Saëns was an influence on other French composers, including **Gabriel Fauré**. The younger man took over from Saint-Saëns as organist at the Church of La Madeleine in Paris.

Although Fauré's talent was nowhere near as prodigious as his mentor, he was also a fine pianist. He was not a wealthy man, and needed his job as organist, choir master and teacher to pay the bills. That meant relegating composition to his spare time but, despite this, he clocked up well over 250 published works. Some of these were a long time in their gestation: Fauré's *Requiem* took more than 20 years to write.

In 1905, Fauré was made director of the Paris Conservatoire and was accorded the status necessary

for him to have a big say in the development of French music at the time. He retired 15 years later and struggled with his hearing late in life.

Today, Fauré is well respected outside France, although his music remains far more popular there than elsewhere.

At a glance: Edward Elgar

Born: 1857
Died: 1934
Nationality: English
Must listen: *Enigma Variations*; *Cello Concerto*; *Chanson de Matin*; *Pomp and Circumstance March No. 1*; *Pomp and Circumstance March No. 4*; *Salut d'Amour*; *Serenade for Strings*

You can hear an excerpt from *"Nimrod"* from the *Enigma Variations* on **CD Track 19**. See page 197 for more information.

For fans of English music, the arrival of **Edward Elgar** must have been something of a relief. Many music historians regard him as the first significant English composer since Henry Purcell way back in the Baroque period, although we did stop off at Arthur Sullivan on our journey through classical music history.

Elgar loved England dearly, particularly his native Worcestershire, where he spent most of his life,

taking the beautiful countryside of the Malvern Hills as his inspiration.

Elgar's childhood was steeped in music: his father ran the local music shop in Worcester and was the organist at the local church. The young Elgar was taught the instrument by his father and by the time he was 12 years old, he was already the reserve organist at church services.

After a year working in a solicitor's office, Elgar decided to try to make his way in the far less financially secure world of music. He worked as a jobbing musician for a while, giving violin and piano lessons, playing the violin in local orchestras, and even doing a little conducting.

Gradually, Elgar's reputation as a composer grew, although it was a hard slog for him to break through into the public consciousness outside of the area in which he lived. It was his *Variations on an Original Theme* that did the trick. This work is now better known as the *Enigma Variations*.

Elgar's music is now seen as being intensely English, and his work is often called into play at major national events. His *Cello Concerto* has a sense of the English countryside about it; *"Nimrod"* from the *Enigma Variations* is often played at times of national remembrance; and his *Pomp and Circumstance March No. 1* is more commonly

known as *"Land of Hope and Glory"*, which is performed at "Proms" concerts all over Britain every year.

Elgar was a private man who loved family life. He did, however, leave behind one other magnum opus – his big, bushy moustache. You can see it for yourself on the back of any £20 sterling note. Apparently, the detail of his whiskers makes the notes particularly hard for counterfeiters to copy.

At a glance: Giacomo Puccini

Born:	1858
Died:	1924
Nationality:	Italian
Must listen:	*"Che Gelida Manina"* and *"O Soave Fanciulla"* from *La Bohème*; *"O Mio Babbino Caro"* from *Gianni Schicchi*; *"Un Bel Di"* and *The Humming Chorus* from *Madam Butterfly*; *"Nessun Dorma"* from *Turandot*; *"Vissi d'Arte"* from *Tosca*

You can hear an excerpt from *La Bohème*, on **CD Track 20**. See page 197 for more information.

Back in Italy, **Giacomo Puccini** was the natural heir to Giuseppe Verdi at the top of the Italian opera composers' league.

Puccini's family had always been involved in church music, but after he saw a performance of Verdi's

Aida, Puccini found the call of the opera too great to ignore.

After studying in Milan, Puccini's first big operatic success was *Manon Lescaut* in 1893. After that, he had success after success after success: *La Bohème* in 1896, *Tosca* in 1900 and *Madam Butterfly* in 1904.

In all, Puccini composed 12 operas, with *Turandot* his final one. He died with just a small part of the work still unwritten. This was completed by another composer but, at its premiere, the conductor Arturo Toscanini stopped the orchestra playing exactly at the point where Puccini stopped composing. He turned to the audience and said:

Here, death triumphed over art.

With Puccini's death and the premiere of *Turandot*, the Italian operatic composing tradition was also snuffed out. There are no more great Italian opera

---

At a glance: Gustav Mahler

Born:	1860
Died:	1911
Nationality:	Austrian
Must listen:	*Symphony No. 1 ("The Titan"); Symphony No. 2 ("The Resurrection") Symphony No. 5* – particularly the *Adagietto; Symphony No. 8 ("The Symphony of a Thousand")*

composers to come in our *Friendly Guide*. Who knows if the tradition will be rekindled again with a new, as yet undiscovered, talent in the future?

Gustav Mahler's fame during his lifetime was as a conductor rather than a composer. He tended to do the former during the winter and the latter during the summer.

The story goes that as a boy, Mahler discovered a piano in his grandmother's attic. Just four years later, at the age of ten, he gave his first public performance.

Mahler studied at the Vienna Conservatory, where he began composing. In 1897, he became conductor of the Vienna State Opera, a job he would hold with great success for the next ten years.

Mahler himself began to write three operas, although he never finished any of them. Today, we think of him as one of the great composers of symphonies. He is responsible for one of the big blockbusters of the genre, his *Symphony No. 8*, which has more than 1,000 musicians taking part in one way or another: as part of the orchestra, the enormous choir or as solo singers.

After his death, Mahler's music was out of fashion for nearly 50 years before it was revived in Britain and the USA in the second half of the 20th century.

At a glance: Richard Strauss

Born: 1864
Died: 1949
Nationality: German
Must listen: *Also Sprach Zarathustra*; *Der Rosenkavalier*;
             Four Last Songs

Born in Germany, **Richard Strauss** was not part of the Viennese Strauss dynasty (pages 114–115). Although he lived for almost the whole of the first half of the 20th century, he is still regarded as one of the great German Romantics. His international standing fell when he decided to continue working in Germany after 1939, although he was acquitted of being a Nazi collaborator at the end of World War Two.

Strauss was a fine conductor, which allowed him to develop an intimate understanding of just how orchestras worked. He put this insight into practice throughout his career as a composer. He was also keen to pass on his experience to other conductors, saying:

Never look at the trombones, it only encourages them.

and:

Don't perspire while conducting, only the audience should get warm.

Strauss is best remembered today for the opening to *Also Sprach Zarathustra*, which was used in the Stanley Kubrick film *2001: A Space Odyssey*, but he wrote some fine operas – among the best to come from Germany ever – including *Der Rosenkavalier*, *Salome* and *Ariadne auf Naxos*. He also composed the very beautiful *Four Last Songs* for voice and orchestra just a year before he died. They were not actually the last songs that Strauss wrote, but they serve as a fitting finale to his composing career.

At a glance: Jean Sibelius

Born: 1865
Died: 1957
Nationality: Finnish
Must listen: *Karelia Suite*; *The Swan of Tuonela*;
              Finlandia; *Valse Triste*; *Violin Concerto*;
              Symphony No. 5

So far, the only major Scandinavian composer to feature in our *Friendly Guide* has been the Norwegian, Edvard Grieg. We return to Scandinavia now, and home in on Finland, where **Jean Sibelius** became a national musical hero.

Sibelius's music is infused with Finnish folk mythology. His greatest work, *Finlandia*, is seen by Finnish people as being as musically representative of them as the English see many of Elgar's works today. Sibelius was, like Mahler, also regarded as a master of the symphony.

133

Away from music, Sibelius was a heavy drinker and smoker, and he suffered from throat cancer in his forties. He was also hopeless with money and was given a state pension so that he could continue composing without having to worry about his finances. More than 20 years before his death, Sibelius stopped composing any music at all. He lived out the rest of his days in a fairly solitary state. He had particularly strong views on those who were paid to comment on his work:

Pay no attention to what the critics say. No statue has ever been put up to a critic.

At a glance: Sergei Rachmaninov

Born: 1873
Died: 1943
Nationality: Russian
Must listen: *Piano Concerto No. 2*; *Piano Concerto No. 3*; *Rhapsody on a Theme of Paganini*; *Symphony No. 2*; *Vocalise*

Our final Late Romantic composer is another man who lived until the middle of the 20th century, and he actually composed many of his biggest hits in the 1900s. Yet he is still considered to be a Romantic composer – in fact, for our money, he was the most Romantic of the lot.

Sergei Rachmaninov was born into a family that was not as well off as it had once been. As a child, his musical talents were recognized and he was sent off to study, first in St Petersburg and then in Moscow.

Rachmaninov was a stunningly good pianist, and developed as a fine composer, writing his *Piano Concerto No. 1* when he was just 19. He also found time to pen his first opera, *Aleko*.

Rachmaninov was never the happiest soul, and many photographs show him looking decidedly grumpy in front of the camera. It was something that his fellow Russian composer, Igor Stravinsky, noticed:

Rachmaninov's immortalizing totality was his scowl. He was a six-and-a-half-foot-tall scowl . . . he was an awesome man.

When Rachmaninov played for Tchaikovsky, the older man was so impressed that he gave him an "A++++" on his score sheet – the highest marks ever given in the Moscow Conservatory's history. Rachmaninov quickly became the talk of the town.

Nevertheless, things were not to go so well for Rachmaninov for too long. When his *Symphony No. 1* was premiered, it received a terrible panning from the critics and Rachmaninov sank into a deep

depression. His work rate slowed considerably, and he started to have trouble composing anything at all.

In the end, Rachmaninov went to see a hypnotherapist called Dr Nikolai Dahl, who managed to set Rachmaninov back on the road to recovery. And, by 1901, Rachmaninov finished the piano concerto that he had been trying so hard to write for ages. He dedicated his work to Dr Dahl, and it was regarded as a triumph by Russian audiences. The new work was his *Piano Concerto No. 2*, which has been a favourite of classical music lovers across the world ever since.

Rachmaninov began to tour across Europe and to the USA. When he was in Russia, he continued working as a conductor and a composer. Following the Russian Revolution in 1917, Rachmaninov took his family off on a tour of Scandinavia. He never went back home. Instead, he moved to Switzerland, where he had a house on the banks of Lake Lucerne. He had always loved rivers and boats and was, by now, a rich man.

Rachmaninov was a brilliant conductor and he had this advice for those who also wanted to excel in this field:

A good conductor ought to be a good chauffeur. The qualities that make the one also make the other. They

are concentration, an incessant control of attention, and presence of mind – the conductor only has to add a little sense of music.

In 1935, Rachmaninov decided that he would make even more of a fortune by returning to the USA. First he lived in New York, before finally moving to Los Angeles. Once he was there, he set about building himself a new home that was absolutely identical to the one he had left behind in Moscow.

As he grew older, Rachmaninov conducted less and less – and composed hardly at all. It was as a pianist that he reached the height of his fame.

Despite missing his homeland, Rachmaninov enjoyed everything that the USA had to offer. He was incredibly proud of his large Cadillac, and often offered to drive guests home from his house, just so that he could show it off.

Just before he died, Rachmaninov became an American citizen. He was buried, not in Russia, but in his new homeland, in New York.

The end of the Romantic period

We have dedicated more pages of our *Friendly Guide* to the Romantic period than to any other era of classical music. There was so much music being written in so many different places that the musical

commentators of the time must have had trouble keeping up. There was a real change in the sound of classical music in this period, with the most popular composers ending up writing music with big, rich, lush orchestral sounds. In many ways, Rachmaninov best exemplifies this. When you think back to a composer such as Beethoven, who was still writing music at the start of the Romantic period, it's easy to see just how much things changed.

However, if you think the sound of classical music changed during the 80 or so years of the Romantic period, then that is nothing to what happened afterwards. In the next period of classical music, things really started to sound very different – and not always for the better, either, in our opinion.

06

The 20th Century

Modern . . . or what?

We are back to that issue of trying to label classical
music again, and its stubborn resistance to being
categorized into a series of boxes. The composers that
we cover in this chapter of our *Friendly Guide* were
all writing music in the 20th century, and many
books would consider them to be "modern" or
"contemporary" composers. However, we're not quite
sure that this sort of label is appropriate any more.

Consequently, we have divided the next two
chapters into the 20th century and the 21st century,
with those composers who have been writing music
since the year 2000 in the second category.

For this reason, we are not convinced that we should refer to composers who have been dead for more than 70 or 80 years as being "contemporary" or "modern". Maybe somebody will come up with a better title for these composers one day, but in the meantime we are gathering them under the heading "The 20th century".

What else was going on in the world?

This was the century when the world became the place that we know now. Telephones, radios, televisions, widespread car ownership, international air travel, space exploration, home computers, compact discs, the internet – all of these inventions changed the way people lived their lives.

Two world wars had a huge impact on society and international relations. This century also saw a change in the world order, with the USA and Russia taking on superpower status.

At a glance: Claude Debussy

Born:	1862
Died:	1918
Nationality:	French
Must listen:	*Clair de Lune*; *La Mer*; *Prélude à l'Après-midi d'un Faune*

Our first 20th-century composer, **Claude Debussy**, was an innovator through and through. He was responsible for changing all sorts of rules about how classical music should be written. Debussy lived in Paris, which was going through a phase of being at the very centre of classical music development during his lifetime.

While he was studying, Debussy showed a precocious talent for composing music with harmonies that were completely out of the ordinary. He is seen as an "Impressionist" composer, and spent much of his time with the painters who were grouped together under the same heading.

Debussy took the inspiration for his music from paintings, works of literature and the artists who lived around him in his flat in the Montmartre district of Paris. He was particularly fascinated with all things oriental.

Debussy had a complicated private life, with two of his lovers attempting to shoot themselves when he began relationships with new women. Towards the end of his life, he fought a long battle with cancer. By the time he finally succumbed to the disease, Debussy had achieved widespread international fame.

Debussy's music was so different that when you listen to it and compare it with what had come

before, it is easy to understand why he is seen as something of a torch-bearer for those composers who followed.

At a glance: Erik Satie

Born: 1866
Died: 1925
Nationality: French
Must listen: *Gymnopédies*; *Gnossiennes*

Another Frenchman, **Erik Satie**, took individualism in his music to the absolute extreme.

It would be fair to say that Satie was an odd man, and this was reflected in the titles he gave to some of his works: *Veritable Flabby Preludes (for a Dog)*; *Sketches and Exasperations of a Big Boob Made of Wood*; *Five Grins or Mona Lisa's Moustache*; *Menus for Childish Purposes*; *Three Pear-Shaped Pieces* [there were seven of these]; *Waltz of the Chocolate Almonds*; and *Things Seen from the Right and Left without Spectacles*.

One of Satie's strangest compositions is called *Vexations*. It is made up of the same few bars of music, which are played over and over again a total of 840 times. Unsurprisingly, this has never proven to be a big concert hall hit, although every so often it is given an outing – usually more as a publicity stunt than a serious concert performance.

Satie's idiosyncrasies are also apparent in his ballet, *Parade*, which features parts for typewriter, whistle and siren. All this madness aside, he did write some beautiful solo piano works, including his famous *Gymnopédies*, although his sister Olga, who knew him as well as anyone, should probably have the last word on Erik:

My brother was always difficult to understand. He doesn't seem to have been quite normal.

At a glance: Maurice Ravel

Born:	1875
Died:	1937
Nationality:	French
Must listen:	*Boléro*; *Pavane pour une Infante Défunte*; *Daphnis and Chloé*; *Piano Concerto in G, Hand*; *Le Tombeau de Couperin*

We stay in France for our third composer of the 20th century. **Maurice Ravel** achieved unimaginable fame thanks to the decision by Jayne Torvill and Christopher Dean to choose his *Boléro* as their musical accompaniment as they skated their way to an Olympic gold medal and into the British sporting hall of fame in 1984.

Another "impressionist" composer, Ravel's music was often clubbed together with that of Debussy. He was also a musical innovator and, again like

Debussy, he did not always see eye to eye with the French musical establishment.

A brilliant pianist, Ravel composed widely for the instrument, but for many people his ballet *Daphnis and Chloé* is his greatest work, despite the famous *Boléro* threatening to eclipse it in the public's mind.

Ravel was a short man and was not allowed to fight in World War One. Instead, he worked as an ambulance driver and was deeply affected by the scenes of carnage that he witnessed. The sadness he felt is mirrored in the music he wrote at the time, such as the very moving *Le Tombeau de Couperin*.

At a glance: Ralph Vaughan Williams

Born:	1872
Died:	1958
Nationality:	English
Must listen:	*Fantasia on a Theme of Thomas Tallis*; *The Lark Ascending*; *English Folk Songs Suite*; *Fantasia on Greensleeves*; *Symphony No. 2* ("*London*"); *Symphony No. 5*

Leaving the eccentricities of France behind, we travel back across the Channel to England, to a man who must rank alongside Edward Elgar as the most English of composers.

Ralph Vaughan Williams was born in the very quaint sounding Gloucestershire village of Down Ampney. A pronunciation note before we get started: Vaughan Williams's first name rhymes with "safe".

Vaughan Williams began collecting traditional English folk songs from a young age. He used these tunes later in life as the central plank of many of his greatest successes. He studied at the Royal College of Music in London, at the same time as Gustav Holst. The two became lifelong friends.

Vaughan Williams wrote nine symphonies, six operas, and a ballet, as well as numerous hymn tunes and scores for stage and screen. His music has deservedly seen a steady increase in popularity over the past 20 years, with *The Lark Ascending*, which is written for violin and orchestra, proving to be particularly popular among Classic FM listeners. This piece is similar to many of his other works in the way in which it manages to paint a picture of the English countryside.

By the way, Ralph Vaughan Williams was not the only famous name in his family – his uncle was the great Charles Darwin.

Another Gloucestershire boy, **Gustav Holst** was born in Cheltenham, where his father was an organist and piano teacher.

At a glance: Gustav Holst

Born: 1874
Died: 1934
Nationality: English
Must listen: *The Planets Suite; St Paul's Suite*

Holst was of Swedish descent, and his full name was Gustavus von Holst. He became concerned during World War One that he might be mistaken for being German, so he shortened his name.

A trombonist by trade, Holst turned out to be a very gifted teacher and, for many years, he was Director of Music at St Paul's School for Girls in London. He drew upon English folk tunes for the inspiration for many of his works, although he was also inspired by subjects as far apart as astrology and the poetry of Thomas Hardy. Asked about his composing, Holst said:

Never compose anything unless not composing it becomes a positive nuisance to you.

It is easy to think of him as a "one-hit wonder" today because of the enormous success of his *Planets Suite*. Six of the seven movements represent the astrological influences of the planets: Mars (war), Venus (peace), Jupiter (jollity), Uranus (magic), Saturn (old age) and Neptune (mysticism). Mercury, the winged messenger of the gods, is the

star of the other movement. You will notice that Pluto is not included in this list. The reason is simple – the planet had not been discovered at the time that Holst composed the work. Although *The Planets* is often performed as a complete work, *"Jupiter"* has a life all of its own as the tune to the great English rugby hymn *"I Vow to Thee my country"*.

At a glance: Frederick Delius

Born: 1862
Died: 1934
Nationality: English
Must listen: *La Calinda*; *On Hearing the First Cuckoo in Spring*; *The Walk to The Paradise Garden*

The third of our trio of 20th-century English composers is Bradford's most famous son, **Frederick Delius**. His father was a prosperous wool merchant who didn't like the idea of his boy following a career in music. In an attempt to distract him from composing, Delius was sent to run an orange plantation in the USA. This actually had the opposite effect and inspired Delius to write *Appalachia*, which relies on African-American spirituals as its core.

While he was in the USA, Delius took lessons from an American organist, Thomas F. Ward. When he

returned to Europe, Delius's father gave up fighting his son's musical aspirations and the young man was sent to study in Leipzig.

After that, Delius moved to Paris, where he spent much of the rest of his life. While he was there, he contracted syphilis, the symptoms of which made his life particularly unpleasant some 30 years later. He relied on a young Yorkshireman, Eric Fenby, to transcribe his final works.

Much of Delius's music is as English as it is possible for a piece of music to be. Take *Brigg Fair – An English Rhapsody*, for example. This set of variations is based on a folk song that hails from Lincolnshire.

At a glance: Arnold Schoenberg

Born: 1874
Died: 1951
Nationality: Austrian
Must listen: *Verklärte Nacht*

Now, our next composer is somebody that it's impossible not to have a view about. Some people would say he should not appear in this book at all; others would say he is one of the greatest of all composers of the 20th century. Few people who have heard his music have no opinion at all.

Arnold Schoenberg never really made it as a wildly popular composer among ordinary concert goers, but he was very influential and widely admired by other composers.

At first, Schoenberg wrote pieces in the Romantic style, but then he developed a totally different way of composing, with a wholly new set of rules. Previously, composers had written music in various keys or sets of keys, with guidelines governing areas such as harmony and melody. These guidelines also had the effect of maintaining a gentleman's distance from dissonant or discordant music. Schoenberg threw these rules out of the window, in favour of a strict regime whereby no one note could be repeated until all other 11 notes had been played. (There are 12 notes in any one scale.) This equality between all 12 notes – called 12-tone music, or **serialism** – often resulted in jarring or discordant music.

We play very little of Schoenberg on Classic FM because our listeners tell us that they don't like it. However, we have included him in our *Friendly Guide* because he was without doubt an incredibly important figure in 20th-century classical music, although the tunes he wrote are definitely an acquired taste.

It's important to stress that although other composers were influenced by Schoenberg, by no means all of them wrote music like him.

At a glance: Béla Bartók

Born: 1881
Died: 1945
Nationality: Hungarian
Must listen: *Concerto for Orchestra*

There is only one other great Hungarian composer whom we cover in detail in our *Friendly Guide* – the marvellous piano virtuoso Franz Liszt. But **Béla Bartók** wrote music that was far more Hungarian-sounding than his predecessor. In fact, Hungarian folk music became the abiding passion of Bartók's life.

Together with his great friend and fellow composer **Zoltán Kodály**, Bartók criss-crossed the country, gathering recordings of authentic Hungarian tunes on a primitive machine, which imprinted the sounds on wax cylinders. The two men kept careful records of everything they heard, producing one of the finest recorded archives of any country's music. Before this, tunes were passed from person to person and were not written down anywhere. As no recordings had previously been made, many of these tunes would have died out completely had it not been for the efforts of Bartók and Kodály.

Bartók became a music professor in Budapest, but he decided to leave the country with the onset of World War Two. He took up a job at an American

university, where he composed and gave piano concerts. Once there, he was not the hit he had been in his homeland and, in 1945, he died of leukaemia. Bartók left behind one particularly interesting work, his *Concerto for Orchestra*. Usually concertos are for a solo instrument and an orchestra, rather than for the whole group of instruments, but Bartók believed that the Boston Symphony Orchestra, for whom it was written, was so great that it deserved to have a concerto composed for solo groupings from within the orchestra.

At a glance: Igor Stravinsky

Born: 1882
Died: 1971
Nationality: Russian
Must listen: *The Rite of Spring*; *The Firebird*

Igor Stravinsky was a giant among 20th-century composers. He was always keen to innovate and was often at the forefront of new trends in the way that classical music was written.

Stravinsky was lucky enough to have Nikolai Rimsky-Korsakov as his teacher when he was a boy. He never received any other formal instruction in how to compose.

As an adult, Stravinsky's talents were spotted by the great impresario, Sergei Diaghilev, who had the

power to make or break composers. Diaghilev commissioned Stravinsky to write *The Firebird*, which was based on an old Russian folk story. It was a big hit.

Stravinsky's next commission from Diaghilev was *Petrushka* – another ballet and another massive critical and box office success. Things didn't go so well when the two men paired up once again though. Stravinsky's *Rite of Spring* caused mayhem at its premiere, with a riot quite literally breaking out in the audience. This was not just murmurings of discontent, but full-on fighting. Half the audience were outraged by what they heard and the other half recognized Stravinsky's talent for innovation and were prepared to defend the work.

Stravinsky moved from Russia to Switzerland, and then to France, and finally to the USA, where he set up home, first in Hollywood and then in New York. He had never been afraid to reinvent himself musically, and his writing changed in style considerably over the years. At times he was particularly radical and during other periods he was more conformist to the classical music norms. These chameleon-like qualities extended to Stravinsky's life away from music as well. Along the way, he managed to change his nationality three times.

Stravinsky was always ready with a witty one-liner, whether talking about other composers, his

audiences or just classical music in general. You will find him quoted in other places in our *Friendly Guide*, but here are two of his sayings that remain personal favourites:

Too many pieces of music finish too long after the end.

To listen is an effort, and just to hear is no merit. A duck hears also!

At a glance: Sergei Prokofiev

Born:	1891
Died:	1953
Nationality:	Russian
Must listen:	*Romeo and Juliet*; *Lieutenant Kijé Suite*; *Peter and the Wolf*; *Classical Symphony*; *The Love for Three Oranges*

Another giant of 20th-century Russian music, **Sergei Prokofiev** was one of the many composing whizz-kids that we have featured in our *Friendly Guide*. In his case, he had managed to clock up two whole operas by the time he was 11.

After studying at the St Petersburg Conservatory, where he made a name for himself as a very challenging modernist composer, Prokofiev continued to write music that, to be frank, shocked his audiences. Like Stravinsky, he too was commissioned to write two ballet scores by

153

Diaghilev, but neither enjoyed the great success of Stravinsky's big hits.

Prokofiev decided to move to the USA after Lenin took control in Russia, and he achieved major success as a concert pianist. He was commissioned to turn his piano work *The Love for Three Oranges* into an opera. It had a rocky beginning, but has eventually become one of his best-loved pieces – and certainly his most successful opera.

In 1936, Prokofiev decided to return home to Russia, but his timing was terrible as his arrival coincided with the period in which the state started to dictate what composers could and could not write. At one stage, Prokofiev faced charges of composing music that worked against the state, but he battled through.

It seems a rather cruel irony that Prokofiev died of a brain haemorrhage on the same day that Stalin – the man who had done so much to oppress his music over the years – also died.

At a glance: Francis Poulenc

Born:	1899
Died:	1963
Nationality:	French
Must listen:	*Gloria*; *The Story of Babar, the Little Elephant*; *Organ Concerto*

You may have seen this man's name on the side of pharmaceutical products because **Francis Poulenc**'s father was a wealthy chemist who owned the family firm Rhône-Poulenc.

Poulenc was the most famous of a group of French composers who were known as "Les Six". (The others were **Darius Milhaud, Germaine Tailleferre, Arthur Honegger, Louis Durey** and **Georges Auric**.)

Poulenc became well known for his ballet *Les Biches,* and then for a long series of popular French songs. His composing style changed, though, following the death of a friend. He became more religious and his music reflected his new-found faith. This period saw him write a number of religious works, including his magnificent *Gloria.*

Poulenc is also known to generations of children as the composer of *The Story of Babar, the Little Elephant.* It remains as good a way as any of introducing youngsters to classical music.

At a glance: George Gershwin

Born: 1898
Died: 1937
Nationality: American
Must listen: *Rhapsody in Blue*; *Piano Concerto in F*; *Porgy and Bess*; *An American in Paris*

Our next trio of pre-war composers were all
from the USA. Although we have
mentioned the USA many times so far in our
Friendly Guide – particularly during the Romantic
period – we have not yet featured any American
composers.

Probably the biggest earner of all classical composers
in his own lifetime, **George Gershwin** was banking
as much as US$250,000 a year, which was no mean
feat in the 1930s.

Gershwin wrote a succession of very successful
Broadway shows, film scores and orchestral works.
A virtuoso pianist himself, he toured the USA and
Europe.

With a background in writing hit musicals,
Gershwin knew a good tune when he heard one, and
his orchestral works, such as *Rhapsody in Blue* and
An American in Paris, have show-stoppingly tuneful
moments. His opera *Porgy and Bess* includes songs
such as *"Summertime"* and *"I got Plenty o' Nuttin'"*,
which are still performed with great regularity today.

They say that opposites attract, and one of
Gershwin's fans was none other than Arnold
Schoenberg. It is hard to think of two men who
wrote more contrasting music. In fact, the two
played tennis together.

At a glance: Aaron Copland

Born: 1900
Died: 1990
Nationality: American
Must listen: *Fanfare for the Common Man*; *Rodeo*;
               Appalachian Spring, including the traditional
               "Shaker" tune *Simple Gifts*

Our next composer holds the distinction of being the only composer so far to have lived entirely in the 20th century. The son of New York Jewish immigrant parents, **Aaron Copland** was a musically talented teenager who decided he could learn more by studying in Paris. By the time he returned to New York, he had an idea that he wanted to develop a truly American sound to his music. Although it was without doubt classical music that he wrote, Copland managed to blend in elements of jazz and folk music.

Copland wrote a series of blockbuster ballet scores including *Billy the Kid*, *Rodeo* and *Appalachian Spring* – all of which are now regarded as being as American as apple pie. His *Fanfare for the Common Man* features at the inauguration of the President of the United States of America. Not bad for a guy whose parents were from Russia and whose original surname was Kaplan.

After World War Two, Copland changed his writing style and started to adopt the "serialism" advocated

by Schoenberg. The pieces he wrote in this period
of his life were nowhere near as popular as those
that had come before, although he did once say:

*Composers tend to assume that everyone loves music.
Surprisingly enough, everyone doesn't.*

At a glance: Samuel Barber

Born:	1910
Died:	1981
Nationality:	American
Must listen:	*Adagio for Strings*; *Violin Concerto*

Samuel Barber composed music that was Romantic
in style, long after the Romantic period had
disappeared. In fact, he was born in the year when
we consider the Romantic period to have ended
altogether.

Barber was not an innovator like Schoenberg,
Stravinsky or Copland, and he certainly didn't write
big showy tunes like Gershwin. Instead, he wrote
memorable melodies – but not too many of them –
with only around 50 of his works published during
his lifetime.

Barber is chiefly remembered today for his *Adagio
for Strings*, which was used by Oliver Stone in his
Vietnam War movie, *Platoon*; and for his *Violin
Concerto*, which gives the soloist a particularly tough
workout in its final movement.

At a glance: Joaquín Rodrigo

Born: 1901
Died: 1999
Nationality: Spanish
Must listen: *Concierto de Aranjuez*; *Fantasía Para un Gentilhombre*

Something of a "one-hit wonder", **Joaquín Rodrigo** is famous for his *Concierto de Aranjuez*. He composed extensively for the guitar, although he was not actually a guitarist himself. His music did much to make it acceptable to treat the guitar as a serious classical instrument, performing alongside the orchestra. Rodrigo was helped in this mission by two excellent exponents of his work – the British guitarist Julian Bream and the Australian guitarist John Williams. (Don't confuse this John Williams with the American composer of the same name; we meet the latter on page 179.)

Rodrigo's music is filled with sunny Spanish tunes and, although he is remembered in the main for just one piece, his output was prodigious. He became blind at the age of three years, and composed all of his music using Braille. He always said that, had he not been blind, he would never have become a composer.

William Walton took over Edward Elgar's crown as the English composer that the establishment loved

At a glance: William Walton

Born:	1902
Died:	1983
Nationality:	English
Must listen:	*Spitfire Prelude and Fugue*; *Crown Imperial*; *Orb and Sceptre*; *Belshazzar's Feast*; *Viola Concerto*; *Façade*

the most. Born in Oldham, Walton spent a good deal of his childhood at Christ Church, Oxford, where he was a boy chorister. After studying music at Oxford University, he was lucky enough to find himself taken under the wing of the Sitwell family, an artistic and literary tribe, who took care of all of his financial needs, allowing him to compose without having money worries.

When Walton was 19, he wrote *Façade* as an accompaniment to Edith Sitwell's rather outlandish and highly theatrical poetry. In his twenties, he wrote two of his other most important works – his *Viola Concerto* and *Belshazzar's Feast*, a breathtaking oratorio, which was premiered in Leeds.

Walton became a renowned film composer in the 1940s, and his Shakespearean collaborations with Laurence Olivier were particularly admired. He also wrote music such as *Crown Imperial* and *Orb and Sceptre* for major state occasions.

In 1948, Walton and his wife left Britain and moved to the island of Ischia, where she still lives today. If you are ever on the island, do make time to visit the very beautiful gardens at their home.

At a glance: Dmitri Shostakovich

Born:	1906
Died:	1975
Nationality:	Russian
Must listen:	*Jazz Suites Nos. 1* and *2*; *Romance* from *The Gadfly*; *The Assault on Beautiful Gorky*; *Symphony No. 5*; *Piano Concerto No. 2*

Dmitri Shostakovich was another composer who, like William Walton, wrote a whole body of film soundtracks, including the very famous *Romance* from *The Gadfly* and the less well known, but terrifically dramatic, *The Assault on Beautiful Gorky*.

Shostakovich was also a graduate of the St Petersburg Conservatory, where his *Symphony No. 1*, written while he was still a student, was hailed as a masterpiece. He fell foul of the state in 1934, though, when Stalin stormed out of a performance of his opera *Lady Macbeth of the Mtsensk District*. The review in the following day's *Pravda* read: "Chaos instead of Music". And the reviewer went on to brand Shostakovich as: "An enemy of the people".

Shostakovich penned his *Symphony No. 5*, which is subtitled *"A Soviet Artist's Practical Creative Reply to Just Criticism"*, as a way of trying to get back into favour. It worked, and he was welcomed back into the fold, although he still had run-ins with the authorities later in his career, and he was only really creatively free once again when Stalin died in 1953.

Shostakovich's music could be light and frothy, for example, his *Jazz Suites*; or dark and dramatic, for example, his *Symphony No. 7*. This epic work tells the story of the siege of Leningrad by the German army.

One interesting aside: Shostakovich also holds the distinction of having one of his songs sung by the cosmonaut Yuri Gagarin over the radio from his spacecraft to mission control down on planet earth.

At a glance: John Cage

Born:	1912
Died:	1992
Nationality:	American
Must listen:	It's tough stuff – give his *Sonatas* and *Interludes* a listen and you'll see what we mean.

Our next composer falls into the same category as Schoenberg. **John Cage** is not somebody whose music we often play on Classic FM. Again, this is

because our listeners tell us that they are not overly fond of it. However, he was a big figure in 20th-century classical music, so he does deserve a mention in our *Friendly Guide*.

Cage was one of the major experimentalists of classical music. He made it his life's work to explore different sounds that did not follow any of the rules that had developed over the years that this book covers. His music could be completely simple, or terribly complicated and chaotic.

Cage even created a new instrument – a "prepared piano" – where pieces of metal and rubber are inserted into the body of the piano to create a completely different sound. He also used electronic tape in some of his pieces.

Cage's most notorious work is called *4'33"* and is made up of four and half minutes of absolute silence, where a pianist sits staring at the piano keyboard without playing a note. The "music" is then supposed to be whatever other noises are heard in the background in the concert hall. Those in the know hailed this as a magnificent concept. We think they may have missed out on having the story of the *Emperor's New Clothes* read to them when they were children.

Born in Lowestoft, **Benjamin Britten** had a consuming love of the county of Suffolk,

At a glance: Benjamin Britten

Born: 1913
Died: 1976
Nationality: English
Must listen: *The Young Person's Guide to the Orchestra*;
             Four Sea Interludes from *Peter Grimes*;
             Ceremony of Carols

spending the last 30 years of his life in the seaside village of Aldeburgh, where he began the Aldeburgh Festival. This is still one of England's annual musical highlights today. Britten lived with his lifelong partner, the tenor Peter Pears, for whom he wrote leading roles in many of his works.

Britten specialized in writing opera and vocal music, with the opera *Peter Grimes*, and his *War Requiem*, written for the opening of Coventry Cathedral, being among his most highly regarded works. However, his most widely heard piece today could not be more different. *The Young Person's Guide to the Orchestra* was written as an introduction to each section of the orchestra for children for a documentary film made by the Crown Film Unit. Its correct name is actually *Variations and Fugue on a Theme of Henry Purcell* – and the theme in question was taken from the incidental music that Purcell wrote for a play called *Abdelazer*.

Britten provided one of the best analogies we have seen to describe how composers go about their business:

Composing is like driving down a foggy road toward a house. Slowly, you see more details of the house – the colour of the slates and bricks, the shape of the windows. The notes are the bricks and mortar of the house.

Even though Britten was the first composer to be made a Life Peer, he could be surprisingly unstuffy about what life as a composer was really like:

The old idea . . . of a composer suddenly having a terrific idea and sitting up all night to write is nonsense. Night time is for sleeping.

At a glance: Leonard Bernstein

Born:	1918
Died:	1990
Nationality:	American
Must listen:	*Candide*; *Chichester Psalms*; *West Side Story*

A larger than life character and a brilliant musician, **Leonard Bernstein**'s big tuneful hits could not have been more different to those written by his fellow American, John Cage.

Bernstein was an accomplished pianist and a brilliant conductor, touring the world, working with

the best orchestras, and spending 11 years as the principal conductor of the New York Philharmonic Orchestra. Bernstein was a master of composition and could as easily write a big populist Broadway hit such as *West Side Story*, as he could create a beautifully poignant choral work such as *The Chichester Psalms*.

Bernstein was also the first composer to become a television and radio star, and he hosted regular "Young People's Concerts" for much of his life.

When Bernstein conducted major concerts, his assistant would stand in the wings with a glass of whisky in one hand, a towel in the other, and a lit cigarette in his mouth. As soon as Bernstein finished his performance, he would rush off stage covered in sweat. He would grab the towel and wipe his face; down the scotch in one; and then take a huge drag on the cigarette, before charging back into the hall to rapturous applause from his adoring public.

The 21st Century

Today's best music

You could argue that the division between 20th-century and 21st-century composers is a purely arbitrary one. It would be true to say that many of the composers who follow enjoyed great success during the 20th century. However, we wanted to make a distinction in our *Friendly Guide* that you will not find in many other histories of classical music.

All of the composers we feature in this chapter have composed a significant body of work in the 20th century. All of them have also made a contribution to 21st-century classical music, so we believe that,

with the benefit of historical perspective, divisions between 20th-century and 21st-century composing may well be made. We're too close in terms of time to be sure where the musical historians of the future will place the dividing line between the end of one period of classical music and the beginning of the next, but we are sure that this line will be drawn, just as it has been in each of the periods we have covered in this book, right back to Early Music times.

At a glance: Peter Maxwell Davies

Born:	1934
Nationality:	English
Must listen:	*Farewell to Stromness*

When **Peter Maxwell Davies** was made Master of the Queen's Music in 2004, he followed a long line of illustrious composers in the job, including Edward Elgar.

Known to everyone simply as "Max", Davies studied at the Royal Manchester College with a group of young British composers, such as **Harrison Birtwistle**, who were together labelled the "Manchester School".

Davies studied in Italy and the USA before returning to England as a school teacher. During his long career, he has written many works specifically

for performance by school children. As well as an opera, *Taverner,* based on the life of the John Taverner we heard about back in Chapter 2 of our *Friendly Guide,* he has also written a stunning *Antarctic Symphony,* based on the time he spent literally at the end of the world.

Desolate landscapes must particularly appeal to Davies because he has lived on Orkney since 1971, with the island and the sea providing huge musical inspiration over the years since. One of his most popular works among Classic FM listeners is *Farewell to Stromness,* a solo piano piece written as a protest against a nuclear reprocessing plant on one of the Orkney Isles.

At a glance: Henryk Górecki
Born: 1933
Nationality: Polish
Must listen: *Symphony No. 3; Totus Tuus*

The fame of **Henryk Górecki** rests on one particular work, his *Symphony No. 3,* which has the subtitle *"Symphony of Sorrowful Songs".* The recording made by the soprano Dawn Upshaw and the London Sinfonietta proved to be a massive hit back in 1992, when Classic FM began broadcasting. The words sung by the soprano, which Górecki sets to music in the second movement of this symphony, were written on a cell wall of the Nazi Gestapo's

headquarters by a young girl in World War Two. The result is achingly beautiful and can be extraordinarily moving for the listener.

In the early part of his career, Górecki wrote many pieces that were quite experimental in their sound and very different to his later work. He has a strong religious belief, which has particularly come to the fore in his music in recent years.

One quick note on his surname: it's not pronounced as it looks. The correct way of saying it is "Goretski".

At a glance: Arvo Pärt

Born: 1935
Nationality: Estonian
Must listen: *Spiegel im Spiegel*; *Cantus in Memoriam Benjamin Britten*; *Fratres*; *Tabula Rasa*

If we were to start to try and identify "schools" from within our 21st-century composers, then we would find that Henryk Górecki's music sits very comfortably alongside that of **Arvo Pärt** and **John Tavener**. All three men have made their names by composing ethereal sounding choral music, which has its roots in their religious faith. Their CD releases have been commercially successful, but this has come about more through listeners making a spiritual connection with the music than through any form of rampant consumerism on the part of the composers.

Pärt's earlier work was quite a tough listen, but in 1969 he stopped composing altogether for seven years after joining the Russian Orthodox Church. When he started writing again, his music took on the style that we know and love today. With its very clean, crisp sound, it has a sparseness about it, which makes it hauntingly beautiful – and extremely relaxing as well.

At a glance: John Tavener

Born: 1944
Nationality: English
Must listen: *The Protecting Veil*; *The Lamb*; *Song for Athene*

Another religious man, **John Tavener** is a member of the Orthodox faith. His music draws on the traditions of Christian Orthodoxy, as well as Islamic and Indian music.

Remarkably, Tavener owes some of his early success to Ringo Starr. Tavener's brother was doing some building work for the legendary drummer and gave him a copy of Tavener's *Celtic Requiem*. Starr liked it so much that it was released on the Beatles' own Apple record label.

Tavener's music reached its widest audience many years later in 1997 when his *Song for Athene* was used at the funeral service held at Westminster Abbey for Diana, Princess of Wales.

Tavener often composes with a particular performer in mind, and he has written a number of works specifically for the soprano Patricia Rozario to sing. *The Protecting Veil*, one of his relatively few non-vocal works, was written for the cellist, Steven Isserlis.

We have said it before, but it bears saying again. Don't confuse him with the John Taverner who was born in 1490. The clue to who is who is in the spelling.

At a glance: Philip Glass

Born:	1937
Nationality:	American
Must listen:	*Violin Concerto*; *Koyaanisqatsi*; *The Hours*; *Kundun*

During his long and distinguished career, **Philip Glass** has been successful at just about any type of classical music he has turned his hand to.

Glass studied at the Juilliard School in New York and also in Paris, before spending time learning about Indian music, a tradition that continues to fascinate him.

Glass is one of the driving forces behind **minimalism**, alongside **Steve Reich** and **Terry Riley**. This style of music is deceptively simple, often with a few notes repeated over and over again. The effect can be totally mesmerizing for the listener.

Much of Glass's music has been first performed by his own group, The Philip Glass Ensemble, but he has also written for orchestras, with his *Violin Concerto* being by far his most widely heard work. His soundtrack for Stephen Daldry's film *The Hours* was another great success.

At a glance: John Rutter

Born: 1945
Nationality: English
Must listen: *Requiem*; *A Gaelic Blessing*; *For the Beauty of the Earth*; *The Candlelight Carol*; *Shepherd's Pipe Carol*

Enormously popular, **John Rutter**'s music is probably performed more often in more places than any other 21st-century composer. His bright and tuneful choral music has made him particularly famous across Britain and the USA, and he has specialized in writing Christmas music to such an extent that it is now unusual to go to a carol concert and not hear at least one of his works.

Like Peter Maxwell Davies, Rutter has often written music specifically to be performed by youngsters. His *Requiem*, which is arguably his greatest work, has become particularly popular with amateur singing groups, and the printed parts for this work are in constant demand across Britain and the USA.

Based in Cambridge, Rutter founded the Cambridge Singers in 1979. They have since given many of the greatest performances of his work.

At a glance: Karl Jenkins

Born: 1944
Nationality: Welsh
Must listen: *Adiemus: Songs of Sanctuary*; *Palladio*;
Requiem; *The Armed Man: A Mass for Peace*

Another highly commercially successful composer, the Welshman **Karl Jenkins** has written music that Classic FM listeners have taken straight to their hearts. He has been the highest ranked British composer in our annual Classic FM Hall of Fame popularity poll for a number of years (see page 199 for more details).

After studying at the University of Wales and at the Royal Academy of Music, Jenkins began his career performing jazz and was a member of the 1970s band *Soft Machine*. He then moved into writing

music for television adverts, winning many awards in the process.

It is as a classical composer that Jenkins is now famed. *Adiemus: Songs of Sanctuary* was the work that first propelled him to the top of the charts – a rare feat for any contemporary classical composer. Its catchy and instantly recognizable style made this fusion of choral and orchestral music a success around the world – it has notched up 17 platinum or gold album awards. Recently, *Adiemus* has been eclipsed by another of Jenkins's works, *The Armed Man: A Mass for Peace*, which has a particularly beautiful cello solo in its *"Benedictus"*.

At a glance: Paul McCartney

Born: 1942
Nationality: English
Must listen: *Liverpool Oratorio, Standing Stone, Working Classical,* *"Ecce Cor Meum"*

Think **Paul McCartney** and you don't necessarily think "classical composer", but the former Beatle has carved out a successful classical music career alongside his rock and pop work. He has always had a knack for writing highly melodic music, and this is apparent throughout his classical pieces.

McCartney's first full-length foray into the world of classical music came with *Paul McCartney's*

Liverpool Oratorio. This homage to McCartney's home city received its premiere in Liverpool Cathedral in 1991.

McCartney followed this up with *Working Classical,* an album of orchestral and chamber music, and *Standing Stone,* which revisited his earlier successes working with a choir and orchestra. At the end of 2006, McCartney released a new classical work, *"Ecce Cor Meum",* an oratorio in four movements.

An item of trivia for you: extracts from Beethoven's *Symphony No. 9* and Wagner's *Lohengrin* are both included in the Beatles' movie *Help.*

At a glance: Ludovico Einaudi

Born: 1955
Nationality: Italian
Must listen: *Stanze; Le Onde; Eden Roc; I Giorni; Una Mattina; Zhivago*

Ludovico Einaudi not only composes music, but he also gets out on the road and performs it, with a particularly strong fan base in Britain, Germany and his native Italy. He trained in Milan, before being taught by the respected Italian composer Luciano Berio.

Einaudi's popularity is based largely on his solo piano albums, *Le Onde,* which was inspired by

Virginia Woolf's novel *The Waves*, and by *I Giorni*, which followed on from his travels around Africa, particularly in Mali. He has also written soundtracks for a number of Italian films.

At a glance: Joby Talbot

Born: 1971
Nationality: English
Must listen: *The Dying Swan*, *The Hitchhiker's Guide to the Galaxy*, *Once Around the Sun*

The youngest living composer in our *Friendly Guide*, **Joby Talbot** was Classic FM's first ever Composer in Residence. The CD *Once Around the Sun* is the culmination of that year-long project.

A graduate of the Guildhall School of Music and Drama in London, Talbot was a member of the pop band *The Divine Comedy* before turning to composition of classical music, and film and television scores.

Talbot's film work includes scores for Alfred Hitchcock's *The Lodger* and for *The Hitchhiker's Guide to the Galaxy*, with his television work including scores to *Robbie the Reindeer* and *The League of Gentlemen*.

Patrick Hawes took over from Joby Talbot as Classic FM's Composer in Residence in 2006. In

At a glance: Patrick Hawes

Born: 1958
Nationality: English
Must listen: *Blue in Blue*; *Into the Light*

recent years, Hawes has emerged as one of the
most popular contemporary English composers.
His monthly commissions for the radio
station are gathered together on the album *Into
the Light*.

Hawes's debut album *Blue in Blue* made the fastest
ever appearance of any work in the Classic FM Hall
of Fame, entering the upper reaches of the chart just
months after it was released. His beautiful choral
piece *Quanta Qualia* has proven to be a particularly
big hit.

Hawes's music follows the English Romantic
tradition of Delius and Vaughan Williams, although
Hawes has a particular interest in Renaissance and
Baroque music – a subject which he studied at
Durham University.

Hawes has also written for television and the
cinema, most notably the score to *The Incredible
Mrs Ritchie*.

Our final group of 21st-century composers have all
entered the public consciousness principally as

At a glance: John Williams

Born: 1932
Nationality: American
Must listen: *Star Wars*; *Harry Potter*; *Schindler's List*;
             Superman; *E.T.*; *Raiders of the Lost Ark*; *Jaws*

writers of film soundtracks. As you may remember,
back in the introduction to our *Friendly Guide*, we
argued that these composers follow a long tradition
of writing for film, which takes in the likes of Saint-
Saëns, Copland, Vaughan Williams, Walton,
Prokofiev and Shostakovich.

We begin with the undisputed celluloid king. So far,
John Williams has written the music for more than
100 different movies. And there is no doubt that
the rest of the film industry appreciates his talents:
he has 43 Oscar nominations, carrying off the
statuette 5 times; 19 Golden Globe Award
nominations, winning 3 times; and 13 Emmy
Award nominations, with 2 victories. His
mantelpiece must by now need some sort of
structural reinforcement, such is the weight of his
accolades.

Williams was born in New York in 1932, moving
with his family to Los Angeles in 1948. He had
loved music from when he was a boy and, after
finishing his first set of studies, he joined the
American Air Force.

Next, Williams moved back to New York for more studying, this time at the world famous Juilliard School. In the evenings, he made money working as a pianist in many of the jazz clubs in the city's Manhattan area.

Finally, Williams made the move back to Los Angeles, where he started to work in the film and television industry. Throughout the 1960s, he wrote the theme tunes of many successful American television programmes.

Then, in 1973, Williams met the film director Steven Spielberg, with whom he has subsequently enjoyed the greatest creative partnership of his long career. Their first film was called *Sugarland Express*. Since then, their list of credits includes blockbuster after blockbuster. Williams has also collaborated very successfully with the *Star Wars* director, George Lucas, working on all six films in the series.

Despite the fact that he could choose to write his music using a computer programme, Williams prefers the old-fashioned way of composing. He uses a piano to work out the tune, and a pencil and paper to write down what he has composed. It's hard work, too – he might only have eight weeks to write around two hours of music for a full orchestra for a film.

At a glance: John Barry

Born: 1933
Nationality: English
Must listen: *Out of Africa*; *Dances with Wolves*; *The Beyondness of Things*

Britain's answer to John Williams is **John Barry**. Born in York, Barry's father owned a cinema business, and Barry was always fascinated by the movies.

Barry's film soundtracks, spanning more than 30 years include *Zulu*, *The Ipcress File*, *Born Free*, *Midnight Cowboy*, *King Kong*, *The Deep*, *Chaplin* and *Indecent Proposal*.

Barry is probably best known for his work on the James Bond films *From Russia with Love*, *Goldfinger*, *Thunderball*, *You Only Live Twice*, *On Her Majesty's Secret Service*, *Diamonds Are Forever*, *The Man with the Golden Gun*, *Octopussy*, *A View to a Kill* and *The Living Daylights*.

Barry's greatest classical scores are *Out of Africa* from 1985 and *Dances with Wolves* from 1990. It is no accident that both these films feature wide open landscape photography – just the sort of images that blend perfectly with Barry's lush, epic scores. The director of *Out of Africa*, Sydney Pollack, said of John Barry:

You can't listen to his music without seeing movies in your head.

The film earned Barry his fourth Oscar, a Grammy Award for Best Instrumental Composition and a Golden Globe Award. *Dances with Wolves* won him his fifth Oscar and another Grammy Award for Best Instrumental Composition.

The Beyondness of Things was Barry's first album of classical music not written as a film soundtrack. The absence of pictures did nothing to dampen his ability to compose great tunes.

At a glance: Howard Shore

Born: 1946
Nationality: Canadian
Must listen: *The Lord of the Rings*; *Gangs of New York*;
              The Aviator; *Panic Room*; *The Silence of the Lambs*

No list of 21st-century film composers would be complete without mention of the Canadian **Howard Shore**. He wrote the soundtracks to all three movies that make up Peter Jackson's *Lord of the Rings* trilogy.

When we ask Classic FM listeners to vote for their all-time favourite film soundtracks, it is *Lord of the Rings* that consistently tops the poll.

A little dinner party trivia for you: Shore himself is rumoured to make a cameo appearance as a Rohan Guard in the extended DVD edition of *The Lord of the Rings: The Return of the King.*

At a glance: James Horner

Born:	1953
Nationality:	American
Must listen:	*Titanic; Apollo 13; Braveheart; Field of Dreams; A Beautiful Mind; The Perfect Storm; The Missing; The Mask of Zorro; Iris*

Born in America, **James Horner** started playing the piano when he was five years old and trained at the Royal College of Music in London before moving back to California, where he studied for a series of music degrees, culminating in a doctorate in Music Composition and Theory.

Horner's first major film soundtrack was *Star Trek: The Wrath of Khan* in 1982, and since then he has worked with film directors such as Steven Spielberg, Oliver Stone and Ron Howard, scoring more than 100 films.

One of the most commercially successful film composers, Horner has won three Grammy Awards, two Oscars and has a further five Oscar nominations and four Golden Globe nominations to his name. His best-known work by a long, long way is *Titanic.*

At a glance: Hans Zimmer

Born: 1957

Nationality: German

Must listen: *Gladiator*; *Mission Impossible*; *The Last Samurai*; *Rain Man*; *Pearl Harbor*; *Driving Miss Daisy*; *The Lion King*; *My Beautiful Laundrette*

A brilliant musician as a child in Frankfurt, **Hans Zimmer**'s career began in the world of pop music, working with the band *Buggles*. Their hit *"Video Killed the Radio Star"* was the first ever video to be broadcast on MTV.

Zimmer worked as an assistant to Stanley Myers and had early success as the writer of television theme tunes. As a film composer, he has made his name for his skilful combination of electronic music with a traditional orchestral sound. His biggest success has been the soundtrack to *Gladiator*, which has sold more than 3 million copies around the globe.

The future

And so there we end our journey through the history of classical music – a journey that has lasted for more than 1,400 years so far, and we are confident that there is plenty more to come.

We started way back with Ambrose and Gregory sorting out the rules of plainsong, and then we travelled through musical time, taking in the Medieval, Renaissance, Baroque, Classical and Romantic periods along the way, ending up with the music of the past 100 years.

Is classical music struggling to find its place in the 21st-century world? On the contrary, classical music and the people who compose and perform it are in the rudest of health. It's worth noting that, of the 108 composers that we've featured in detail in our *Friendly Guide*, 54 were alive at some point in the past 100 years. That sounds to us like an art form that is continuing to reinvent itself and to thrive.

The music of the great composers, such as Bach, Mozart and Beethoven, is as relevant to our lives right now as it was on the day that it was written. One of the most exciting parts of life in the classical music industry is the thrill of discovering a work of brilliance, which you can then share with other people. All the time new composers are coming along, writing new pieces that will become central parts of books just like this in the future.

Classical music is a living, breathing entity that will go on changing its shape and sound for as long as there are people with ears to listen.

Have a Listen for Yourself

It would be utterly impossible to fit all of the examples of the different types of classical music onto one CD. The disc that accompanies this book will give you a taster of just some of the music discussed over the preceding pages.

Each of the excerpts has deliberately been chosen from full-length recordings on the Naxos label. All Naxos discs are released at a budget price and represent excellent value for money, so you will be able to experiment and build up your classical library without too much financial risk.

From the early music period

1 Anonymous: *Gregorian Chant*

Pope Gregory I lent his name to this type of music after spending time sorting out and tidying up 6th-century church music. For more details, see page 19.

CD Track 1 is an excerpt from the *Proper of the Mass: Introitus – Adorate Deum*, taken from Naxos 8.550711.

If you enjoy this, then try more anonymous Gregorian Chant – this time sung by female voices: *Ego sum Resurrectio* (Naxos 8.553192).

2 Hildegard of Bingen: *"O Ignis Spiritus"*

Musician, poet, diplomat, visionary, this 11th-century nun had it all. For more details, see page 21.

CD Track 2 is an excerpt taken from Naxos 8.550998.

If you enjoy this, then try Hildegard of Bingen's *"O Viridissima Virga"* and other medieval carols (Naxos 8.550751).

3 Palestrina: *Missa "Papae Marcelli"*

This piece was the result of a test to prove that religious texts really could be understood when they were set as polyphonic music. For more details, see page 29.

CD Track 3 is an excerpt taken from Naxos 8.550573.

If you enjoy this, then try Palestrina's *Missa "L'Homme Armé"* (Naxos 8.553314).

From the Baroque period

4 Purcell: *"When I Am Laid in Earth"* (*Dido's Lament*) from *Dido and Aeneas*

A beautiful lament sung by Dido just after she has discovered that she is not going to be reunited with the love of her life, Aeneas. For more details, see page 42.

CD Track 4 is an excerpt taken from Naxos 8.553108.

If you enjoy this, then try Purcell's *Suites for Harpsichord* (Naxos 8.553982).

5 Vivaldi: *The Four Seasons*

Probably the best known of all Baroque pieces.
If you have only come across this particular
extract, then do make sure that you explore
the rest of the concerto. For more details, see
page 45.

CD Track 5 is an excerpt from the first movement
of *Spring*, taken from Naxos 8.550056.

If you enjoy this, then try Vivaldi's *Concerto for Two
Mandolins RV 532* (Naxos 8.553028).

6 Handel: *"Zadok the Priest"*

Written for the coronation of King George II.
For more details, see page 52. This
triumphant anthem also happens to be the first
piece of music ever broadcast on Classic FM,
just after six o'clock in the morning on
7 September 1992.

CD Track 6 is an excerpt taken from Naxos
8.557003.

If you enjoy this, then try *"The King Shall Rejoice"* –
another of Handel's Coronation Anthems (also on
Naxos 8.557003).

7 Johann Sebastian Bach: *Brandenburg Concerto No. 2*

This is one of six concertos dedicated to Christian Ludwig, Margrave of Brandenburg – although he may never have actually heard them himself. For more details, see page 48.

CD Track 7 is an excerpt taken from Naxos 8.554607. Listen out for the particularly stunning trumpet part.

If you enjoy this, then try Johann Sebastian Bach's *Brandenburg Concerto No. 3* (also on Naxos 8.554607).

From the Classical period

8 Haydn: *"Surprise" Symphony No. 94*

Haydn wanted to startle his aristocratic audience, who often nodded off while listening to the musical entertainment that followed a large meal where the wine had flowed in copious amounts. He lulled them into a false sense of security with a quiet section first, before a thundering chord jolted them from their post-prandial slumbers. For more details, see page 62.

CD Track 8 lets you hear the "Surprise" in its full glory. It is taken from Naxos 8.553222.

If you enjoy this, then try Haydn's *"Farewell"*
Symphony No. 45 (also on Naxos 8.553222).

9 Mozart: *Clarinet Concerto in A*

Written shortly before Mozart died, this piece has
always been a firm favourite. It was used to
particularly good effect in the film *Out of Africa*.
Mozart composed the piece for his good friend,
Anton Stadler, whose playing he admired
enormously. It's worth remembering that in
Mozart's day, the clarinet was longer and heavier
than the modern instrument. So playing this piece
back then required particular dexterity. For more
details, see page 68.

CD Track 9 is an excerpt from the second
movement, taken from Naxos 8.550345.

If you enjoy this, then try Mozart's *Bassoon Concerto*
(also on Naxos 8.550345).

10 Beethoven: *Symphony No. 5*

De-De-De-Derr. De-De-De-Derr. It's the most
famous opening of any piece of classical music, and
over the years all sorts of theories have been put
forward to explain the significance of those opening
few bars. The most popular is that this is the sound
of fate knocking on the door, although a less
mystical explanation is that it is in fact the sound of

Beethoven's grumpy cleaner knocking to be let in. Whatever the truth, it makes for a cracking start to the symphony. For more details, see page 73.

CD Track 10 is an excerpt from the very start of the first movement, taken from Naxos 8.553476.

If you enjoy this, then try Beethoven's *Symphony No. 9* (Naxos 8.553478).

From the Romantic period

11 Paganini: *Violin Concerto No. 1*

Probably the most gifted violin player of his generation, Paganini thrilled crowds across Europe with his total control of the instrument. He knew his own musical strengths, and many of his own compositions, such as this one, were written specifically to allow him to show off his own talents to their best effect. For more details, see page 83.

CD Track 11 is an excerpt from the climax of the *Violin Concerto*, taken from Naxos 8.550649.

If you enjoy this, then try Paganini's *Violin Concerto No. 2* (also on Naxos 8.550649).

12 Chopin: *Prelude No. 15 ("The Raindrop")*

Chopin's piano music included *Ballades*, *Etudes* (studies), *Impromptus*, *Nocturnes*, *Mazurkas* and *Polonaises* (the last two allowing him to indulge in an exploration of the folk tunes of his native Poland). This prelude is a good example of Romantic imagery – close your eyes and listen. You can hear the tiny raindrops falling in the music. For more details, see page 92.

CD Track 12 is an excerpt taken from Naxos 8.553170.

If you enjoy this, then try Chopin's *"Minute Waltz"*, which in fact takes about a minute and a half to play (also on Naxos 8.553170).

13 Bizet: *"The Pearl Fishers Duet"*

Taken from the opera *The Pearl Fishers*, this duet (*"Au Fond du Temple Saint"* to give its correct title) is one of the most popular songs for a tenor and a baritone anywhere in opera. The opera itself is eclipsed by Bizet's *Carmen*, but this particular duet stubbornly remains at the top of every chart of Classic FM listeners' operatic favourites. For more details, see page 96.

CD Track 13 is an excerpt from *"The Pearl Fishers Duet"*, taken from Naxos 8.553030.

If you enjoy this, then try Bizet's *Carmen* (Naxos 8.660005-7).

14 Tchaikovsky: *1812 Overture*

The greatest musical triumph from the pen of one of the most tortured of all composers. Written to celebrate Napoleon's defeat in Russia in 1812, this work is now very popular at outdoor concerts during the summer, with fireworks adding to the cannon that boom out towards the end. If you have the opportunity to go to one of these concerts, do take the children along. They love the spectacle that goes along with an outdoor performance of the *1812 Overture*. By the way, if you're thinking that an overture usually comes at the beginning of an opera or ballet and highlights all the best tunes that you're about to hear, then you would be right. However, this is an example of the other sort of overture, which is a complete piece in its own right. For more details, see page 103.

CD Track 14 is an excerpt from the thrilling climax of the *1812 Overture*, taken from Naxos 8.550500.

If you enjoy this, then try Tchaikovsky's *Romeo and Juliet* (Naxos 8.555923).

15 Johann Strauss Jr: *By The Beautiful Blue Danube*

The best-known waltz of all time, written by the man they called "the Waltz King". For more details, see page 114.

CD Track 15 is an excerpt from *By the Beautiful Blue Danube*, taken from Naxos 8.550152.

If you enjoy this, then try Johann Strauss Jr's *Thunder and Lightning Polka* (on Naxos 8.552115–16).

16 Bruch: *Violin Concerto No. 1 in G Minor*

He may not really be remembered for much else, but Classic FM listeners took Max Bruch to their hearts because of this piece of music. It was the surprise choice in the number one spot when we first began compiling listeners' votes for the Classic FM Hall of Fame back in 1996. It remained at the pinnacle of the chart for another four years, before being dislodged by Rachmaninov and his *Piano Concerto No. 2*. For more details, see page 123.

CD Track 16 is an excerpt from the beginning of the third movement, taken from Naxos 8.550195.

If you enjoy this, then try Bruch's *Symphony No. 3* (on Naxos 8.555985).

17 Verdi: *The "Anvil Chorus"* from *Il Trovatore*

If you have spent any time watching opera, you will know that the storylines can sometimes be illogical. Well, *Il Trovatore* must surely be a contender for the title of "most baffling of the lot". This particular chorus sees a group of travelling blacksmiths bashing away at their forges in time to the music as they belt out one of Verdi's biggest tunes. For more details, see page 117.

CD Track 17 is an excerpt taken from Naxos 8.554707.

If you enjoy this, then try another of Verdi's great operas, *Aida*, (Naxos 8.554706).

18 Richard Wagner: *The Ride of the Valkyries*

Taken from the opera *Die Walküre* (one of the four operas that made up *The Ring Cycle*), this piece depicts fierce warrior women from Scandinavian mythology riding through the sky on horseback. It was also used to particularly good effect as the American helicopters swooped into Vietnam in the film *Apocalypse Now*. For more details, see page 118.

CD Track 18 is an excerpt taken from Naxos 8.550211.

If you enjoy this, then try the *Overture* to Wagner's opera *Die Meistersinger* (Naxos 8.554682).

19 Elgar: *Enigma Variations*

Each of the movements in the *Enigma Variations* depicts one of Elgar's friends. There are two "enigmas": the identity of the "original" theme, and the identities of the friends. There are all sorts of theories as to what the theme might be, but Elgar took the secret to his grave. For more details, see page 127.

CD Track 19 is an excerpt from the ninth variation, *Nimrod*, which depicts Elgar's publisher, August Jaeger, taken from Naxos 8.553564.

If you enjoy this, then try Elgar's stirring *Cockaigne Overture* (Naxos 8.550489).

20 Puccini: *"O Soave Fanciulla"* from *La Bohème*

This is an opera that is full to the brim with great tunes. If you have never sampled a live opera performance before, then **La Bohème** is the perfect choice. In this particular duet, the two love interests, Rodolfo and Mimi, sing together in the moonlight. For more details, see page 129.

CD Track 20 is an excerpt taken from Naxos 8.553151.

If you enjoy this, then try the incredibly famous "*Nessun Dorma*" from another of Puccini's 12 operas, *Turandot* (Naxos 8.550497).

The Classic FM Hall of Fame Top 100

Every year since 1996, we have asked our listeners to vote for their three favourite pieces of classical music. We assemble all of the votes together to create *The Classic FM Hall of Fame Top 300*. This chart is a living, breathing snapshot of our listeners' tastes, and has now become the biggest annual survey of classical music anywhere in the world.

The Top 100, which is listed below, provides an excellent variety of classical pieces for you to explore:

01 Vaughan Williams: *The Lark Ascending*

02 Elgar: *Cello Concerto*

03 Rachmaninov: *Piano Concerto No. 2*

04 Mozart: *Clarinet Concerto*

05 Beethoven: *Piano Concerto No. 5 ("The Emperor")*

06 Elgar: *Enigma Variations*

07 Bruch: *Violin Concerto No. 1*

08 Beethoven: *Symphony No. 6 ("Pastoral")*

09 Beethoven: *Symphony No. 9 ("Choral")*

10 Vaughan Williams: *Fantasia on a Theme by Thomas Tallis*

11 Grieg: *Piano Concerto*

12 Jenkins: *The Armed Man (A Mass for Peace)*

13 Pachelbel: *Canon in D*

14 Sibelius: *Finlandia*

15 Barber: *Adagio for Strings*

16 Beethoven: *Symphony No. 7*

17 Rachmaninov: *Symphony No. 2*

18 Beethoven: *Symphony No. 5*

19 Dvořák: *Symphony No. 9 ("New World")*

20 Mozart: *Requiem*

21 Allegri: *Miserere*

22 Rodrigo: *Concierto de Aranjuez*

23 Handel: *Messiah*

24 Shostakovich: *Piano Concerto No. 2*

25 Tchaikovsky: *1812 Overture*

26 Ungar: *The Ashokan Farewell*

27 Rachmaninov: *Piano Concerto No. 3*

28 Tchaikovsky: *Piano Concerto No. 1*

29 Smetana: *Má Vlast*

30 Mendelssohn: *Violin Concerto in E minor*

31 Holst: *The Planets*

32 Saint-Saëns: *Symphony No. 3 ("Organ")*

33 Bizet: *The Pearl Fishers*

34 J.S. Bach: *Concerto for Two Violins in D minor*

35 Beethoven: *Piano Sonata No. 14 ("Moonlight")*

36 Beethoven: *Violin Concerto*

37 Rachmaninov: *Rhapsody on a Theme of Paganini*

38 Gershwin: *Rhapsody in Blue*

39 Mozart: *Piano Concerto No. 21 ("Elvira Madigan")*

40 Mascagni: *Cavalleria rusticana*

41 Fauré: *Requiem*

42 Handel: *Zadok the Priest*

43 Tchaikovsky: *Swan Lake*

44 Rimsky-Korsakov: *Scheherazade*

45 Elgar: *Pomp and Circumstance No. 4*

46 Vivaldi: *Four Seasons*

47 Tchaikovsky: *Symphony No. 6 ("Pathétique")*

48 Mahler: *Symphony No. 5*

49 Sibelius: *Symphony No. 5*

50 Beethoven: *Symphony No. 3 ("Eroica")*

51 Debussy: *Clair de Lune*

52 Mozart: *Flute and Harp Concerto*

53 Fauré: *Cantique de Jean Racine*

54 Elgar: *The Dream of Gerontius*

55 Shore: *The Lord of the Rings*

56 Widor: *Symphony No. 5 ("Organ")*

57 Albinoni: *Adagio in G Minor*

58 Sibelius: *Karelia Suite*

59 Mozart: *Laudate Dominum*

60 Morricone: *Gabriel's Oboe*

61 Tchaikovsky: *Symphony No. 5*

62 Shostakovich: *Romance* from *The Gladfly*

63 Handel: *The Arrival of the Queen of Sheba* from *Solomon*

64 Mendelssohn: *Hebrides Overture ("Fingal's Cave")*

65 Chopin: *Piano Concerto No. 1*

66 J.S. Bach: *Brandenburg Concertos*

67 Butterworth: *The Banks of Green Willow*

68 Mozart: *The Magic Flute*

69 Einaudi: *Le Onde*

70 J.S. Bach: *Toccata and Fugue in D Minor*

71 Prokofiev: *Romeo and Juliet*

72 Mahler: *Symphony No. 2 ("Resurrection")*

73 Borodin: *In the Steppes of Central Asia*

74 Verdi: *Requiem*

75 Glass: *Violin Concerto*

76 Sibelius: *Symphony No. 2*

77 Verdi: *Nabucco*

78 Jenkins: *Requiem*

79 Shostakovich: *The Assault on Beautiful Gorky*

80 Mozart: *Ave Verum Corpus*

81 Sibelius: *Violin Concerto*

82 Khachaturian: *Spartacus*

83 Mozart: *The Marriage of Figaro*

84 Ravel: *Boléro*

85 Strauss: *Four Last Songs*

86 Vaughan Williams: *Five Variants of Dives and Lazarus*

87 Hawes: *Blue in Blue*

88 Tallis: *Spem in alium*

89 Wagner: *Tannhäuser*

90 Hawes: *Towards the Light*

91 Elgar: *Violin Concerto*

92 Puccini: *Madame Butterfly*

93 Grieg: *Peer Gynt Suite No. 1*

94 Chopin: *Piano Concerto No. 2*

95 Puccini: *La Bohème*

96 Schubert: *String Quintet in C*

97 Orff: *Carmina Burana*

98 Beethoven: *Romance No. 2 in F*

99 Tchaikovsky: *Violin Concerto*

100 Gounod: *Judex* from *Mors et Vita*

10

What They Said About Each Other

They might have been creative geniuses, but the great composers never held back when it came to sparing the feelings of their colleagues, as shown in this selection of sayings uttered by some of the stars of the classical music world:

Rossini would have been a great composer if his teacher had spanked him enough on the backside.

Ludwig van Beethoven

I played over the music of that scoundrel Brahms. What a giftless bastard! It annoys

*me that his self-inflated mediocrity is
hailed as genius.*

PYOTR ILYICH TCHAIKOVSKY

On Hector Berlioz's *Symphonie
Fantastique*:

What a good thing it isn't music.

GIOACCHINO ROSSINI

Also about Hector Berlioz:

*One ought to wash one's hands after
dealing with one of his scores.*

FELIX MENDELSSOHN

*I'm told that Saint-Saëns has informed a
delighted public that since the war began he
has composed music for the stage, melodies,
an elegy and a piece for the trombone. If
he'd been making shell-cases instead it
might have been all the better for music.*

MAURICE RAVEL

*Listening to the fifth symphony of Ralph
Vaughan Williams is like staring at a cow
for 45 minutes.*

AARON COPLAND

205

On hearing John Cage's *4'33"*, which comprises no music, just four and a half minutes of silence:

I look forward to hearing his longer works.

IGOR STRAVINSKY

Wagner has lovely moments but awful quarters of an hour.

GIOACCHINO ROSSINI

One can't judge Wagner's opera Lohengrin *after a first hearing, and I certainly don't intend hearing it a second time.*

GIOACCHINO ROSSINI

Too many pieces of music finish too long after the end.

IGOR STRAVINSKY

Modern music is as dangerous as cocaine.

PIETRO MASCAGNI

Classical Music Used in Films

Classical music and the cinema have been inextricably linked since the earliest days of film.

Today, many contemporary composers have made their names through their film soundtrack work, as we discovered in Chapter 6. However, movie directors have never just limited themselves to commissioning new music when much of the old stuff adds drama or evokes an emotion in a particular scene. So much classical music is used in films that it has become one of the easiest ways for people to listen to classical music without even realizing it.

So, if you are planning to indoctrinate someone you know in the ways of all things classical, you could do worse than renting a few of the DVDs on this list:

20000 Leagues under the Sea – J.S. Bach: *Toccata and Fugue in D Minor*

2001: A Space Odyssey – Richard Strauss: *Also Sprach Zarathustra*

Ace Ventura: Pet Detective – Mozart: *Eine Kleine Nachtmusik*

An American Werewolf in London – Ravel: *Daphnis and Chloé*

Apocalypse Now – Wagner: *Ride of the Valkyries*

As Good As It Gets – Gershwin: *An American in Paris*

Babe – Saint-Saëns: *Symphony No. 3*

A Beautiful Mind – Mozart: *Piano Sonata No. 11*

Bend It Like Beckham – Puccini: *"Nessun Dorma"* from *Turandot*

Billy Elliot – Tchaikovsky: *Swan Lake*

Brassed Off – Rodrigo: *Concierto de Aranjuez*

Bridget Jones's Diary – Handel: *Hallelujah Chorus* from *The Messiah*

Captain Corelli's Mandolin – Puccini: *"O Mio Babbino Caro"* from *Gianni Schicchi*

Catch Me If You Can – Haydn: *Piano Concerto No. 11*

Chariots of Fire – Allegri: *Miserere*

A Clockwork Orange – Beethoven: *Symphony No. 9*

Dead Poets Society – Beethoven: *Piano Concerto No. 5*

Driving Miss Daisy – Dvořák: *Song to the Moon* from *Rusalka*

The Elephant Man – Barber: *Adagio*

The English Patient – Bach: *Aria* from *Goldberg Variations*

Four Weddings and a Funeral – Handel: *Arrival of the Queen of Sheba*

The French Lieutenant's Woman – Mozart: *Piano Sonata No. 15*

The Horse Whisperer – Beethoven: *Cello Sonata No. 1*

Indecent Proposal – Vivaldi: *Concerto No. 8* from *L'Estro Armonico*

JFK – Mozart: *Horn Concerto No. 2*

Johnny English – Handel: *Zadok the Priest*

L.A. Confidential – Mendelssohn: *Hebrides Overture*

The Ladykillers – Boccherini: *Minuet*

Lara Croft: Tomb Raider – J.S. Bach: *Keyboard Concerto No. 5 in F Minor*

Mona Lisa – Puccini: *"Love Duet"* from *Madame Butterfly*

Mr. Holland's Opus – Beethoven: *Symphony No. 7*

Mrs. Doubtfire – Rossini: *"Largo al Factotum"* from *The Barber of Seville*

My Big Fat Greek Wedding – Wagner: *Bridal Chorus* from *Lohengrin*

My Left Foot – Schubert: *Trout Quintet*

Natural Born Killers – Orff: *Carmina Burana*

Ocean's Eleven – Debussy: *Clair de Lune*

Out of Africa – Mozart: *Clarinet Concerto*

Philadelphia – Mozart: *Laudate Dominum*

Platoon – Barber: *Adagio for Strings*

Pretty Woman – Vivaldi: *Four Seasons*

A Room with a View – Puccini: *Doretta's Dream* from *La Rondine*

The Shawshank Redemption – Mozart: "*Che Soave Zeffiretto*" from *The Marriage of Figaro*

The Silence of the Lambs – J.S. Bach: *Goldberg Variations*

Sleeping with the Enemy – Berlioz: *Symphonie Fantastique*

The Talented Mr. Ripley – Bach: *Italian Concerto*

There's Something about Mary – Bizet: *Danse Bohémienne* from *Carmen Suite No. 2*

Toy Story 2 – Richard Strauss: *Also Sprach Zarathustra*

Trainspotting – Bizet: *Habanera* from *Carmen*

The Truman Show – Chopin: *Piano Concerto No. 1*

Wall Street – Verdi: "*Questa, o Quella*" from *Rigoletto*

Wayne's World – Tchaikovsky: *Romeo and Juliet*

Who Framed Roger Rabbit? – Liszt: *Hungarian Rhapsody No. 2*

Where to Find Out More

If this book has whetted your appetite to find out more, one of the best ways to discover what you like about classical music is to tune in to Classic FM. We broadcast 24 hours a day across the UK on 100–102 FM and also on DAB Digital Radio and through digital satellite and cable television. You can also listen online at www.classicfm.com. We play a huge breadth of different classical music each week.

If you would like to delve far, far deeper into the subject than we have been able to do in this short book, the universally acknowledged authority on

the subject is *The New Grove Dictionary of Music and Musicians*. The original version was edited by Sir George Grove, with the eminent musicologist Stanley Sadie taking over the reins for this new edition (published in 1995). But be warned – this is a weighty tome, running to 20 hardback volumes with around 29,000 separate articles. You can also access the database online by subscribing to www.grovemusic.com

In truth, this database is far more detailed than most music lovers would ever need; a more manageable reference book is *The Concise Oxford Dictionary of Music*, edited by Michael Kennedy (published by Oxford Reference), or *The Penguin Companion to Classical Music*, edited by Paul Griffiths (published by Penguin). Paul Griffiths has also written *A Concise History of Western Music* (published by Cambridge University Press) – a highly readable discussion of the way classical music evolved over time.

The *The DK Eyewitness Companion to Classical Music*, edited by John Burrows (published by Dorling Kindersley), is a very colourful and reliable source of information on the chronology of classical music. For a slightly quirkier walk through the subject, we recommend *Stephen Fry's Incomplete & Utter History of Classical Music*, which is published by Macmillan and is based on the Classic FM radio series of the same

name, written by Tim Lihoreau. We also hope
that you enjoy the Classic FM book *Classic
Ephemera* by Darren Henley and Tim
Lihoreau (published by Boosey & Hawkes),
which is packed full of classical music facts, stories
and trivia.

Other excellent general guides to classical music
include: *The Rough Guide to Classical Music*, edited
by Joe Staines (published by Rough Guides); *The
Encyclopedia of Music* by Max Wade-Matthews and
Wendy Thompson (published by Hermes House);
Good Music Guide by Neville Garden (published by
Columbia Marketing); *The Chronicle of Classical
Music* by Alan Kendall (published by Thames &
Hudson); *The Lives & Times of The Great Composers*
by Michael Steen (published by Icon); and *The
Lives of the Great Composers* by Harold C.
Schonberg (published by Abacus). If ever you
happen across a copy of Jeremy Nicholas's two
splendid books, *The Classic FM Guide to Classical
Music* (published by Pavilion) and *The Classic FM
Good Music Guide* (published by Hodder &
Stoughton), then you should snap them up. Both
are sadly out of print at the moment.

Three excellent books on the subject of opera
are *The DK Eyewitness Guide to Opera* (published
by Dorling Kindersley); *The Good Opera Guide*
by Denis Forman (published by Phoenix); and
The Rough Guide to Opera by Matthew Boyden

(published by Rough Guides).

For younger classical music lovers or discoverers, *The Story of Classical Music* and *Famous Composers* are both published by Naxos Audiobooks in association with Classic FM. These titles are aimed at 8- to 14-year-olds and contain musical excerpts and CD-ROM elements.

The series of *Classic FM Friendly Guides* published by Hodder Arnold, of which this book forms a part, is growing fast, with *Friendly Guides* to Mozart, Beethoven and Elgar now available.

For up-to-the-minute news on the latest CD releases, *Classic FM Magazine* contains around 150 reviews each month. You might also enjoy reading *The Gramophone*, the magazine that many music enthusiasts regard as the last word in classical music criticism.

The very best way of finding out more about which pieces of classical music you like is by going out and hearing a live performance for yourself. There is simply no substitute for seeing the whites of the eyes of a talented soloist as they perform a masterpiece on a stage only a few feet in front of you. Classic FM has a series of partnerships with orchestras across the country: the Royal Scottish National Orchestra, the Royal Liverpool

Philharmonic Orchestra, the Philharmonia
Orchestra and the London Symphony Orchestra.
To see if they have a concert coming up somewhere
near you, log on to www.classicfm.com and click on
the "Concerts and Events" section.

Happy listening!

Classical Music Mood Chart

Raise Your Blood Pressure

Lower Your Blood Pressure

Rimsky-Korsakov: *Flight of the Bumblebee*

Khachaturian: *Adagio of Spartacus and Phrygia*

Barber: *Adagio for Strings*

Holst: *"Jupiter" from The Planets*

J.S. Bach: *"Jesu, Joy of Man's Desiring"*

Verdi: *"La Donna è Mobile" from Rigoletto*

Tchaikovsky: *"Waltz of the Flowers" from Nutcracker*

Handel: *"Hallelujah Chorus" from Messiah*

Saint-Saëns: *"The Swan" from Carnival of the Animals*

Mozart: *Eine Kleine Nachtmusik* (1st mvt)

Grieg: *"Solveig's Song" from Peer Gynt*

Smetana: *Vltava*

Bizet: *"Seguidilla" from Carmen*

Mozart: *Piano Concerto No. 21* (2nd mvt)

Copland: *"Hoedown" from Rodeo*

Puccini: *"O Mio Babbino Caro" from Gianni Schicchi*

Tchaikovsky: *Andante cantabile from String Quartet No. 1*

Handel: *Arrival of the Queen of Sheba*

Satie: *Gymnopédie No. 1*

Delibes: *"Flower Duet" from Lakmé*

Ravel: *Pavane pour une Infante Défunte*

Strauss, J. Jr: *By the Beautiful Blue Danube*

Pachelbel: *Canon in D*

Vivaldi: *Spring from the Four Seasons* (1st mvt)

Mahler: *Adagietto from Symphony No. 5*

Elgar: *Nimrod from Enigma Variations*

Wagner: *Prelude to Act 3 from Lohengrin*

Fauré: *Pavane*

Elgar: *Salut d'Amour*

216

Index of Composers

The more important references are in **bold** type.

Acknowledgements

No book would ever be possible without a great editor, and in Ginny Catmur at Hodder Arnold, I have been lucky enough to work with the very best. Her enthusiasm for our *Classic FM Friendly Guides* has known no bound. She has lavished an immeasurable amount of care and attention on each of the books in the series.

I am also very grateful to my colleagues at Classic FM who have offered suggestions, help and inspiration during the writing of this book. Particular thanks go to Alex Edwards, Angie McFarlane, Anne-Marie Minhall, Becky Morton, Ben Eshmade, Bob Jones, Brenda Cavilla, Catherine Turner, Catriona Bryden, Charlotte Rosier, Chris

Suckling, David Mellor, Emma Baker, Emma
Oxborrow, Giles Pearman, Henry Kelly, Jamie
Beesley, Jamie Crick, Jane Jones, Janina Nicoll, Jay
Vydelingum, Joanna Wilson, John Brunning, John
Evans, John Suchet, Katharine Gilbertson, Katie
Derham, Kate Smith, Lesley Garrett, Lisa
Duncombe, Mark Forrest, Mark Goodier, Mark
Griffiths, Matt Francis, Myleene Klass, Natalie
Wheen, Nick Bailey, Nicola Bonn, Nigel Gayler,
Oliver Melville-Smith, Paul Kelly, Paul Osbourne,
Philippa Abrahams, Ralph Bernard, Richard E.
Grant, Richard Henning, Rob Weinberg, Russell
Torrance, Sali-Wyn Ryan, Sam Jackson, Sasha
Handover, Simon Bates, Simon Calder, Steve
Orchard, Stuart Campbell, Tim Lihoreau, Tony
Robinson, Val Trendell and Venetia Heesom.

About the Author

Darren Henley began working as a newsreader at Classic FM in 1992, becoming Managing Editor in 2000 and Station Manager in 2004. Since 2006, he has been Managing Director of Classic FM. He has written 16 books about classical music and musicians. He began his career as a journalist at Invicta Radio in Kent and then at ITN.

The Sony Radio Academy Awards, the Arqiva Commercial Radio Awards, the British Radio Awards, the New York International Radio Festival and the United Nations have all honoured his radio programmes. The American Audiobook Publishers Association consecutively named two of his audiobooks for children, *The Story of Classical Music* and *Famous Composers*, as "best original work" in 2005 and 2006. Naxos Audiobooks publish both. *The Story of Classical Music* also won the *Radio Times* Readers' Choice Award at the British Spoken Word Awards in 2005 and was nominated for a Grammy Award.

He is the author of *Classic FM: The Incredible Story of Classical Music – A Friendly Guide for Children* and *The Classic FM Friendly Quiz Book*, and the co-author of *The Classic FM Friendly Guide to Mozart, The Classic FM Friendly Guide to Beethoven* and *The Classic FM Friendly Guide to Elgar*, all published by Hodder Education.

223

CLASSIC *f*M

The INCREDIBLE Story of

Classical Music

A Friendly Guide for Children

DARREN HENLEY

FOREWORD BY HRH THE PRINCE OF WALES

£5.99 ISBN 978 0340 98357 7